BRIDGES NOT WALLS

For Administrative Assistants

Heidi K. Varucene

The events, conversations, and opinions in this book have been set down
to the best of the author's ability, although some names and locations
have been changed to protect the privacy of the individuals.

For more information:
hvarucene@gmail.com
https://www.facebook.com/heidi.varucene

First paperback edition January 2020

Dedicated to and Honoring my Mom
Mina Cory Kahofer

Foreword

Providing excellent medical care and increasingly complex healthcare for patients and their families requires an extensive team of exceptionally caring and dedicated people. Health organizations are complex networks that are vital to the well-being of those they serve. Staff often work in difficult circumstances to deliver increasingly technical services while striving to demonstrate values of integrity, compassion, and excellence. Job expertise aside, all staff are essential to organizational goals of process improvement, safety, customer service, confidentiality, professionalism, empathy, communication, and teamwork. Healthcare professionals understand that every patient is unique and deserving of the highest quality care.

My career in healthcare administration spans 35 years and my experiences have often evolved around the transformation of struggling community hospitals and health systems. My role in healthcare requires me to not only lead an organization but also to serve on the boards of many health care and community service organizations. Through it all I have had the advantage of working with many excellent Assistants, including most recently Heidi, with whom it has been my absolute delight to partner with for over 13 years.

Assistants work to meet the needs and requests of their leaders, so that in our roles we can focus on major hospital initiatives and issues. This responsibility is not only important, it is essential for us to have our organizations accomplish both short- and long-term strategic objectives. All who encounter effective Assistants feel respected and valued. Assistants solve problems, build teamwork, and seek out opportunities to improve communication and operations in managerial offices. They model warm and attentive professional customer service for the entire organization. They are also tireless advocates for the organization.

Bridges Not Walls broaches many topics, but it is, at its core, a book about human connections. Heidi continues to provide the highest caliber of administrative support to the Board and Senior Leadership of our hospital. Her skillset at managing complicated schedules and organizing meetings is beyond compare. She is positive when dealing with difficult situations and skillfully manages to diffuse customer service issues. Her follow up with details is superb and she is highly reliable. Heidi is always about solutions. We depend on her to keep our administrative team organized and she is truly a pleasure to work with. Her sense of humor (and baking skills) keep us all smiling!

I am delighted she has written this book to share her amazing wealth of knowledge and skills with others in similar positions. Enjoy the read.

Warm Regards,
Bob Chaloner

Preface

"Education is for improving the lives of others and for leaving your community and world better than you found it."
–Marian Wright Edelman

It must have been around the year 1996. My Mom would be retiring in one year from her position as Assistant to the Senior Pastor of an ethnically diverse church/preschool/community center in Jackson Heights, Queens, New York, after a career that began there in 1974. I was 31 and three years into my career path in Assistant roles at a community hospital on the east end of Long Island, New York. She had an office; I had an office. The only major difference between our offices was that she always had a bowl of candy right smack on her desk, which amazingly never threatened her appetite for sugar addiction. My candy bowl is strategically placed just far enough away from my desk and should, but thankfully does not, come with a "no option" alarm. Both offices were thoroughfares that linked the public and staff with the administration. We were the gatekeepers to the leaders of our organizations. When time and space allowed, we would touch base by phone and relate. The word *relate* is Latin in origin (mid-16th century from the verb *referre*) and means *brought back*. We each brought back to each other laughter, frustrations, sympathies, a few or more tears (that may have been just me), sometimes suggestions, and always unwavering attention. The quick hang-up was fully understood. But what was really brought back for me was essentially my first exposure to career-based shared communication. I had this gift with her for one year until her retirement. It's only in reflection that I realized the worth of this harmony and the value of this affinity.

Writing this book has taken me for quite a ride. The views and lessons learned were cultivated in times when life was happening with intense challenges, abundant focus, and motivation. Its heart is lit from the unsuspecting treasures that occur when we don't even know it.

"Life is a school, where you learn how to remember, what your soul already knows." –Unknown

Acknowledgements

Thank you initial proofreaders, Kurt-Eric, Marilyn, Barbara-Jo, Leeve, Phyllis, Deborah, and Alan: stepping out to your confidences gave me courage. Thank you front-line team, Geri and Marilyn: our friendship, your support, and our shared understandings are immensely valued. Thank you leadership team, Bob, Robert, Pat, Sharon, Althea, Fred, Kevin, Steve, Robyn and Chris: you all keep me moving, thinking, and smiling. Thank you past Presidents, (the first) John, Peter, Tom (twice over), Annette, and John (who admirably de-energized a forceful downward spiral within 13 months): some ride – eh? Thank you hospital family: we are not to be underestimated. Thank you Shawn: you technically safeguarded my work. Thank you friends: I am more than fortunate. Thank you my four siblings, Lisa, Kurt-Eric, Amy, and Karl: influences and experiences both precious and prized. Thank you 8 ½ year-old niece Cora: your help on my last page/back cover bio so perfect. Thank you Squeege, Lily, Woody, Roxy and Peetre in-my-heart, et al: you surround me without fail so that I always carry on with a warmed heart. Thank you daughter Nicole: your family, work, laughter, and life journey widens my horizon. Thank you daughter Karrin: your book feedback vital at the perfect time, often on-point, and always thought provoking. Thank you, Mom, Dad, and husband Ed: ♥.

Cover: 50" x 20" oil painting by Dad, Kurt Kahofer (photographed by Rachel Siford)

Introduction

Question: What do you get when you anticipate, envision, respond, shake, and pour?

Answer: an optimized Administrative Assistant in today's workforce, ready and not waiting. Let's get down to it.

It's a given – everyone's circumstance is different. The Administrative Assistant's experiences, motives, and methods are as varied as all possible colors on the display spectrum. Business, healthcare, education, entertainment, government, technology – you name it, there are tools, challenges, lessons, opportunities, and basic truths regarding our Assistant role. To survive it, revive it, and heighten it requires skill, willingness, patience, experience, and heart; all borne from a solution-based drive. And let's not forget about our essential peace of mind.

Hello and it is very nice to communicate with all of you, those whom I know, don't, and will. I'm Heidi; twenty-seven years in the healthcare industry that is delineated by one year in Public Relations; three years in Patient Access/Communications; eight years as an Administrative Assistant to the President/CEO, and fifteen years as the Executive Assistant. All valuable in hindsight, especially in my Executive Assistant role, somehow surviving through the ebbs and flows of seven administrations in a ten-year period. Still in the role now and still getting an education every day. Pleased to report that I have my current boss for a bit over thirteen years. In our initial sit-down, when he (aka Number 7) was first appointed President/ CEO, he asked me if I had any questions or concerns. I told him that my concern was that if he stayed for any extended amount of time, I would not know how I would function since I was the master support staff for administrative transitions. Weathering power struggles and fall-out had become my unsolicited forte. When Number 7 applied for the President/CEO position, and the interview process began, I had a job opportunity offer that was well worth considering. I was ready for change. It was decision time and surprisingly, I gambled and headed out on the road committed as Number 7's Assistant. Truth be told - the decision was not entirely a full out crapshoot. His career profile grabbed my attention. Many times over I had coordinated search committee meetings for the President/CEO role and you soon realize that career profiles tend to read annoyingly alike. What caught my attention in his was a note that read, "This candidate leaves his ego at the door". Pause. Hmmmm. Pause. Never saw that before. I would risk curiosity killing this cat. Decision made. Interesting to discover that there is a rejoinder for the idiom *curiosity killed the cat* and it includes this ending: *but satisfaction brought it back*. The cat survives!

My brother Karl once told me that the real journey just begins at the point a martial artist earns a black belt. I'm both fortunate and blessed to experience this analogy with Number 7.

I'm hopeful that my time served counts for something aside from my livelihood and sense of value, both of which I'm incredibly grateful for. This book is my give-back effort for a career drenched in purpose and service. The mission of it is to help you to be able to leave your work day and your mind-set not only prepared for tomorrow but also incited to face it all head on and energetically.

Our Role: So here we are. Administrative Assistants here to support. The origin of the word *support* is rooted in Latin as *sub* (from below) and *portare* (carry) leaving us with *supportare*. In Old French it is *supporter*. In Middle English it carries the definition of *tolerate, put up with*. Smile. Honesty. It can be the case sometimes – yes. Although *support* can and still does mean the Middle English definition, fortunately for us it is also defined as *help, aid, assist*, and all those good things that call us to duty.

"*The purpose of life is not to be happy. It is to be useful, to be honorable, to be compassionate, to have it make some difference that you have lived and lived well.*"
-Ralph Waldo Emerson

As Assistants we listen and respond. We answer emails/phones/texts/alarms/voices and we can often perform like professional jugglers. Throw in another lit torch or two – we got it. We address all drop-in and otherwise scheduled appointments and we move all requests and situations (verbal, written, the anticipated and not) forward. We pace. We bridge. We absorb and we disperse. We are privy to more than we may desire at times, not because we don't care or are not interested but because we are trying to sustain, manage, and hopefully grow our day. We track projects, people, and ourselves. We set an example and raise the bar. No pressure there! And we know we are a critical and necessary part of the team. Our responsibility is enormous, and it is also what we make of it. Good questions to ask ourselves in the private first person . . . really, who am I in my role and what is it that I see for me now and for my tomorrows? Ah yes - time management is key - energy and attention management is paramount - and the all-embracing mind management is essential.

New to the position friends – Welcome and the intention is to offer you some straight lines between point A and point B (or A and Z as can be the case) so that you can bring more of what you have to offer to your work and to your vision. The tangible A through Z points you will find in this book are not new. They do work for me and may offer you some thoughts about your specific situations. There is good tool-type information out there, some in print and much in cyberspace, to streamline our methods. There is psychology-based information out there as well to help us handle situations. I prefer to learn through objective insight into my own state of affairs. This can lead to education via trial and error, but this suits me because I get lost and distracted if the lesson is not brought home and applied. So, it is the abstract in this book that I hope you will benefit from most. The workload and situations we face can indeed be challenging, because life and people can be complicated, fair is not always the case, and add our own life backdrops to those ingredients and we can have the failure or the flourish end result.

Less new to the position friends – Congratulations on all you do so well and a monumental thank you for your influences on the journey. Much of this book may read as obvious to you because we are veterans of experience and exposure. Some twenty plus years ago I remember leaving my home on a Saturday at 6:30am for an 8:00am board of directors meeting, despite that I live just seven minutes from door to door. Meeting materials and logistics were fully prepared throughout the prior week. I won't ever forget my anxiety as I drove to work consciously taking deep, calm breaths while listening to Pachelbel's *Canon in D Major*. There was much to give to my new job and even more to prove to myself. Now I fly into those meetings, well-timed and ready, listening to the likes of GNR's *Welcome to the Jungle* and hoping my hair is dry enough to not look like I just jumped out of the shower. I still have much to prove. It's just more so to myself than others. Note to self: circumstantial times currently exist when I need to break out the classical music or one of my go-to favorites, *You'll Never Walk Alone*, sung by Rene Fleming. As the years have gone by, I remind myself to never forget what it is like to head into unfamiliar territory. So, I hope you enjoy the connection to the learning curves we continue to undergo. We are indeed a spoken and often not spoken unified force. And you are indeed quite incredible people.

The Assistant role is unique – it can be quite unbelievable at times. Although the role risks saturation that can lead to near gridlock, there are great possibilities for us to create our masterpiece on an open canvas.

So much to cover.

Table of Contents

Get ready, get set . . . oh wait . . . one more thing . . . although names (except for in Acknowledgements and in Chapter 14) and locations are changed, ALL stories are absolutely true.

. . . Let's go!

CHAPTER 1

Learn to Love the Calendar * Contacts at their Best * Email Ease

There is no more synergistic relationship than that of the calendar/contacts/email. Maximum efficiency can be achieved when these three tools, each individually refined, join in harmony with each other. Let's first break it down.

Learn to Love the Calendar

The calendar is a heavy-hitter topic. If one item can rouse the blood pressure in an Assistant, it is the calendar. Back in the day, management of this beast of a responsibility would have been the first thing I would have omitted from my duties if I could. The calendar can often be frustrating and can become all consuming. It keeps moving, constantly needing to be fed and changed like a newborn baby. At one point in my career, it mirrored a love/hate relationship and has now evolved into a lucrative investment that has saved me many times over in myriad ways. The calendar is the choreography of the day and sets a tone for us and our bosses. Aside from it needing buffer, office, travel, meeting, and hopefully essential-in-truth break times, it also dictates movement and pacing. This is huge. If worked well, priorities fall on the days and times that are most sensible. It takes a calm, thoughtful mind and good communication skills for this type of calendar condition and momentum to occur. Through the calendar, we have a heavy hand in creating the weather of our workdays.

The calendar deserves complete and accurate attention if we want to reap the benefits of our investment. Requests can come at us like snow in headlights. No judgement there for there is important work going on. There are both individual and organizational reputations to uphold, there are documents to be overnighted that count for progress, and there are communications that need to occur for someone's well-being or for closure to some hard-earned initiative. How ready are we for the snowflake or the hailstorm? Pressures, hyper-expectations, time restraints – those are the times the Assistant can fold . . . or shine. I have heard the best hit tennis ball is the one that takes the least effort. That shot has a whole lot of time and preparation behind it. Same goes for the touchdown, ace, homerun, spike, and the optimized calendar.

Ooooh –yea!   Ooooh –yea!   Ooooh –yea!

What does it look like on the meeting calendar?

Invest in the following: correct spelling of names/companies (because we strive for excellence), primary contact number (because we *will* need it), color code (i.e., conference room use all in purple because visuals are discernible and awesome), consistent acronyms (because we cannot write novels in calendars), location/videoconference/phone notations (because options increase with technology), and relevant notes. Here is the calendar visual:

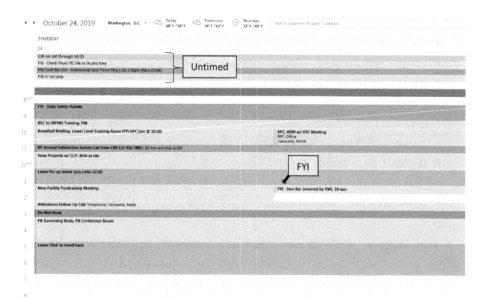

Let's cover relevant notes. I put these in parentheses.

Our boss presents at a recurring monthly orientation meeting. Participation varies from 12 to 50 new hires. Relevant note: (44 expected). Why note it? It is the same orientation that will be given regardless of the number of attendees. Note it because it is part of preparation. Our job is to clear obstacles and prepare ahead, so that our boss can enter with materials in hand and an anticipation of circumstance. Ask the questions. Ask the number of attendees. Waiting for information to come to us can be a misuse of constructive time and supporting facts may not come at all on their own. Being proactive is powerful and has its own chapter (Chapter 9, *Proactive Anticipation during Changing Tides*).

Relevant notes in parentheses work for both our bosses and us, and:

- helps us track: Lunch w/ delegates (location TBD)
- specifies time frames: Conference (7a-5p; you present 2-3p)
- sets status: (cancelled by [company])
- confirms closure: (lunch ordered 5/14)
- alerts action: (see Wednesday folder)
- establishes how: (Ann will pick you up - this entrance at 11:50a)
- shows players: (MBJ, RFR, HKB-will try, SDR on phone)
- notes responsible party: (Amy x 5342)
- directs expectation: (will call here or dial ***-***-****)
- provides specifics: (Oncology/Hematology MD)

The degree and visual ease of relevant information in the calendar will come through for us in both calm and rough waters. Questions and requests abound and we have it covered – one screen – no digging and no need to try to remember.

So, drive stick shift through our calendar entries. We have a lot more ability to respond quickly and accurately. There is an art, which quickly improves with practice, to having this wealth of information on the calendar while keeping it short and to the point. Our investment in this will pay off with a high return rate.

What else can work for us on the calendar?

Calendar View Options. Choose calendar view options that suit us best (day/week/month). I have the day view screen up for the day and I stray from that when determining early morning/late night appointments or day before/day after appointments. I also switch up the calendar view when I need to get my mind straight on what's coming up, when something has already occurred, or when I need to see occurrences in relation to each other.

4

FYIs – Untimed and Timed. FYIs can work well in both the timed and untimed portions of the calendar because FYIs serve to provide our bosses with organizational awareness. They build understanding of the bigger picture scene.

Untimed. The top portion of the calendar in day view is not to be underestimated. It is where valuable, non-specific time information is provided. The line items are found directly under the top-left date (see calendar diagram). For example: FYI – check Thursday folder; FYI – conference room use by Accounts Dept 1-2p; FYI - CPL weekend coverage through 11/2; and let us not forget – FYI – Heidi on vacation through Thurs. (perhaps highlight that one in bright yellow). Set the day's stage; the performance is poised for both understanding and action.

Timed. Entries that *begin* with FYI within the time-portioned of the Calendar (see calendar diagram), let's say blocked from 10:00-10:30, and reads, *FYI- Customer Service Staff Session, Conf Rm 3*, means that our boss's attendance is not required but we want our boss to know that something is occurring. When our boss sees FYI – it is an *immediate* message that it is simply an FYI. If we can equip our bosses with some top to bottom and inside to outside awareness from our point of view, we will have an unspoken, time saving, shared platform to work from. This platform helps to turn fragmentation into integration.

The optimized calendar will save us from having to verbalize information to our boss, which is often not an option anyway given their schedules and their existing focus.

Getting ahead in the calendar is another investment that we can profit from. There are ways to advance while managing our already busy-enough days. We are in the calendar six months out because we are entering travel arrangements for a three-day conference out of state. We enter the information and see the conflicts. Why worry – it is six months down the line and there is plenty on our plates. Choice time – investment opportunity. Pick up the phone (because live time can be immediate closure and human connections must not be forgotten) and reschedule the conflict. We may be met with "When?? You are moving something in June??" Yes. We. Are. Six months of work moves on – June comes – already taken care of. Multiply that type of action by six months' worth of meeting conflict clearing and whatever day we are on is set and free of problems for the most part. Side bonus - the other party's calendar is also void of that conflict.

Speaking of getting ahead, this skill can also be a life preserver when we least expect it and most need it. The following example typifies the beauty of being steps beyond what is current.

A group of state regulators shows up for an unannounced five-day survey visit. Both the administration conference room and the boss calendars are set for the week. Although they are reasonably paced, there is little wiggle room. The previous week we jumped ahead and accomplished payroll even though we could have saved that task for deadline Monday morning. We inventoried and stocked our supplies (paper, postal, kitchenette, cartridges, etc.) and our four top projects were organized and are now poised to resume their attack on progress with closure timelines in both near and far sight. The unexpected government regulators enter Monday morning and plant their flag in our conference room for the week. Our immediate priority becomes that of clearing a week's worth of conference room and boss meetings. There easily goes half of our day, especially difficult since conference rooms are often prime real estate. Here is the point about jumping ahead and being steps beyond. The preparation time we invested in throughout the prior week will result in our paycheck (payroll complete), we can easily get a hot, needed cup of coffee (supplies inventoried), and our top projects bravely await us (project organization). Happy Monday morning. We can now focus on the state regulators absent of low hanging fruit pressures. Why work from defense where we end up in constant catch-up mode when we can operate more comfortably from offense? It is worthwhile to invest in our peace of mind.

How soon should the calendar be established for the upcoming year? For starters, when we have recurring meetings, click on the *no end date option* (unless the meeting is so defined that there is an actual end date). We will establish an indefinite placeholder and if the meeting changes or ends, it is simple to revise or cancel out in just a few clicks. Calendar establishment is ours to determine. I recently read an article in *The Los Angeles Times* titled: *Details Emerge in Deal to Bring 2028 Summer Olympics to Los Angeles.* That is nine years from the point of this writing. Coordination is on-going. It has already begun before prior and current year's events are over. As much as we Assistants work in beginnings, middles, and ends, we also work in broad-view cyclical motion where moving parts are abundant. It is a calm mind can handle both the minutiae and the inclusive.

"Peace. It does not mean to be in a place where there is no noise, trouble or hard work. It means to be in the midst of those things and still be calm in your heart."
-Author Unknown

If we deal with board, leadership, managers, etc., we can figure that calendar planning is underway for all those participants as well. I have found that establishing high-level meetings for the upcoming year is best completed at minimum by September/ October of the current year.

This brings to mind entering holidays into the calendar. We should enter them in there (automatically or manually) as soon as we can and keep a hard-copy list handy for quick reference as we establish the calendar. It is way too easy to overlook these blackout dates while we are keeping so much in motion. It is one thing to relocate a meeting of five, but it is a whole different kettle of fish to move sixty attendees.

Additionally, if our organization has large meetings/events that need to occur, and room capacity consideration is a must (i.e., orientations, trainings, thank you breakfasts, symposiums, recognition celebrations), enter those events as soon as we are able to, both in our boss and conference room reservation calendars. We will be able to ward off conflicts by riding shotgun. *Riding shotgun* was originally used to describe the guard who rode alongside a stagecoach driver, ready to use his shotgun to ward off bandits. I don't know about all of you, but I've been in positions, whether I'm guarding my rights to a conference room or needing to seize someone else's, where instinctually I'm ready to barter with a valuable to secure my flag. Let's just say that finding space solutions for *all* is a more suitable behavior and humor can often bring opposing camps to agreement. If any of you have ever received goods from me, please take it to your grave. Much appreciated.

Contacts at their Best

While calendar is the *what*, clearly contacts are the *who*. Take the time to capture contact information wherever possible throughout our day. Yes, when asked, we can seek out this information and, we do. It is a search, a call or two, maybe three. Tick. Tick. Tick. Hopefully it is not too tedious finding exactly whom we need. This is why the investment in detailed contact information is worthwhile; so that we have it before we even know that we need it. If we are on the phone with someone for whatever reason, let's take a moment to pull up their contact information (enter here we masters of multi-tasking) and take the opportunity to ask for and get what may be missing, like a mobile number, spouse's name, birthdate, conference phone standing dial-in numbers/codes, or whatever it is that we may need down the line. One of the beauties of email is the extensive contact information that usually and automatically comes at the end of an email. Just copy the entire block of contact information and paste it in the notes section of a new contact screen. It is an easy cut and paste to line item at that point, and we will have most everything. At times, I have been tempted to skip the time to do this . . . pressure, pressure, pressure – but it has paid off during trying times when I had more pressure than when I could have cut and pasted. Also, let's not forget to request business cards via email attachment and mobile phone sharing.

Contact information benefits from today's technology. Many of us cover the generations that have straddled us with one foot in what was and the other foot in what is. Then, a dime in a phone booth that we could spot on every corner. Now, the in-hand, infinite-possibility mobile phone knowledge and communication device. This is quite a long jump. I cannot help but think that this extreme existence many of us have is something great to behold. Back to present time, I recently received an off-hours email from a manager requesting an email address for someone whom I was not familiar with, nor whom was in my contacts. My first reaction was to respond that I did not have it, but that I would follow up when I got to the office. Pause. The request came with a clue. The contact in question had attended a meeting the prior day by teleconference. I went to the calendar on my phone and looked at the meeting specifics. In two clicks, I had the person's email information because technology is that intertwined and information that we never entered ourselves can follow a road to our desktop or phone. I forwarded the answer to my very happy colleague. Pushing our own cognitive boundaries will benefit our effectiveness. Point is, there is more than one way to peel an orange. Bigger point – it is ALWAYS about solutions.

Hopefully your organization is moving forward and evolving to new levels and higher standards. Steering committees, forum bureaus, diversity leaderships, working groups, huddles, boards, management huddles, you name it - when we are asked to coordinate a group meeting and we have the foresight that this group will meet again, set up its group distribution list in our contacts *at the onset*. If the title of the group is not clear or determined, take the liberty to determine it and educate all relevant parties on its *specific* title because meetings, sub-meetings, and sub-sub- meetings can all begin to look and sound alike. We best avoid that confusion because it would then become our mess to clean up. For instance, there is a public relations committee (general), a new facility public relations oversight committee (specific) and an ad hoc public relations committee (temporary to address a transition period). Certainly, there is overlapping membership but there are many exceptions. Assistants not only need to be clear and track for themselves but also for all participants who can easily become flummoxed.

Our contacts are forever being perfected. We need to send out an email or an Outlook Invite. Drop in the group distribution list as opposed to repeatedly going through the laborious task of individual entries. Boom . . . done.

Example. A group distribution list in contacts titled *Outpatient Mental Health Facility Group* was created that included eighteen members from two healthcare organizations, a legal firm, public officials and public school leadership. A second group distribution list was created that included only the Assistants related to the participants. This list was titled the same, but *Assistants* followed the title. It is wise to title this way because then both lists appear alphabetically right next to each other in our contacts and both will be needed for correspondence. Some Assistants choose to include the Assistants within one distribution list. I find it more manageable to keep them separate. OK, let's move on with this scenario. Gathering the contact information for all participants took a great deal of time. The group met twice and then ceased to exist. The two distribution lists (participants and Assistants) were deleted in an effort to keep the entire contacts population more current. Over a year went by. One day a very important issue arose that warranted attention. A psychiatrist remembered that a couple of mental health awareness meetings had occurred quite some time ago and so he phoned the Assistant. Point is, meetings that cease, even for a long period of time, can resurface. Save your distribution lists in your contacts. Recreating the two distribution lists would have been nothing short of time consuming and aggravating.

Email Ease

The product from our investment in calendar and contacts is email ease. The email becomes a piece of cake when calendar and contact information are used as basic ingredients. This reminds me of *Grandma's Success Cake* recipe, which is easy to make, easy to freeze and serves up whenever we want. (This recipe can be found at *chefnorway.com/grandmas-success-cake.*) So, let's bake and serve up our emails with ease by using our calendar and contact ingredients.

This email section would be missing a couple of vital organs if it did not address the *reply all* and *high importance* email options that are too often applied and can even become the enemy.

11

Granted, the misuse of *reply all* intentions are . . . well, I often do not know what the intentions are, but I trust they are innocent if not well meant. Goodness help us if they are not.

Here is an enlightening fact. A paid consultant to a municipality sent an email to nine people and it was regarding the potential engagement of one of three reputable firms that would bring an initiative forward. The price tag was high. One of the nine recipients of the email was a Deputy Supervisor (DS), who replied *just* to the consultant sharing his opinion that one of the firms should be omitted from consideration because of sensitive "xyz" reasons. In turn, the consultant *replied all* back to the group of nine, exposing the DS's private opinion that was clearly just meant for him. Short true story - and the consultant was fired the next day.

On a lighter but more annoying note, Assistants are frequently on the receiving end of attendance-taking emails. All are receiving all because of the dreaded *reply all* option. Here is the math. An attendance email is sent to 24 participants. One third of the participants *reply all* back. So, 8 unnecessary emails are sent to 24 people plus 7 Assistants. Get ready - get set - here they come, the march of the attendance responses for a meeting that we are not coordinating. Thanks, but really, no thanks.

Currently, when we click to delete something from our computers, Microsoft sends a pop-up window that says, "Are you sure?", and we reply *yes* or *no*. A good friend suggested to me that Microsoft add the "Are you sure?" pop-up window when we have the option to *reply all*. I reckon he is onto something.

The color gray is a great visual for Assistants to regard because it easily reminds us that nothing in our job description is fixed and there is much beauty that can live between black and white. *Reply all* can, at particular times, work just fine. A president directly emailed two colleagues, also leaders of like organizations, about a dinner meeting that would occur between the three of them the following week. Date and location were determined. The following day the president realized that the dinner location was closed for business (a mistake Assistants usually do not make but have!) for the determined day so *reply alls* transpired. The president copied his Assistant on the original email and so the Assistant had a rare moment to break out the popcorn and watch a streamlined meeting coordination effort occur. Thank you to the bosses of the world who are in the habit of copying their Assistants where appropriate. It is truly appreciated because we can serve you better by you doing so.

The urge to click on the *high importance* option (this sends a red exclamation point to the receiver) on an email is tempting because just about all emails we send are important or we would not be sending them. Using the *high importance* option frequently can fail. Here is why. When I was a kid, my parents bought a grandfather clock. I would hear that clock ring every quarter of an hour and chime the number of hours every hour. This lasted for maybe two weeks. Then I barely noticed the chimes at all because my brain became accustomed to them and ceased to take note. When emails are received from a sender that *always* come with the red alert exclamation point, they actually lose their importance because the brain does not differentiate from levels of urgency and we can cease to take note. When an email is received from a sender who rarely uses the red exclamation point option, and then uses it, it is indeed time to pay attention. This deliberate use of the *high importance* option ties directly to us establishing with others when something is truly pressing. We will then get or give the timely response that we are looking for.

A few words about *forwarding* emails. There are times when forwarding an email to someone makes sense. The information that is being shared needs to be both relevant and appropriate.

Three points of caution. 1. It is presumptuous for us to share a running dialogue between two people with a third party without prior agreement or approval. Respect. The exception to this may be when information is non-specific and inconsequential. 2. Forwarding emails also forwards people's email addresses. Personally, I find this inappropriate. I do not feel comfortable sharing people's contact information (outside of an organization) without their permission first, and I do not want others to assume they can share my contact information either. Chances are, it is not a problem. The problem is the assumption. We always have the option of cutting and pasting just the relevant information and we also have the option to forward an email and utilize the bcc line to honor contact information privacy. Bottom line, technology is magnificent if it does not de-sensitize us to shared mutual respect. People who respect each other trust, support, and value each other's privacy. 3. I imagine we have all been in a position whereby we receive an email forward that asks us to, *Please advise.* We start to scroll down to see what the bottom line is and find pages upon pages of back-and-forth exchanges that are irrelevant to us. *Please advise on what??* Time out. The one thing we do know at this point is that we are not going to start at the very bottom and figure this all out. No . . . will not do. It is a much more productive use of our time to pick up the phone or email back and get the key point, the sum and substance. An email trail can be useful to track the progression of a conversation, but we usually just need the essential point so that we can do what we do best, which is make the next step happen. Our stance on responding to *please advise* email trails will be clear. Use humor. No one is intentionally trying to make us miserable.

Learn to Love the Calendar * Contacts at their Best * Email Ease Wrap-Up

The value of the Assistant is off to a very admirable start when investments are made in the optimization of the calendar, contacts, and email tools. Here are some key takeaways for consideration. Decide to approach calendar management on defense or on offense. Confront the challenge or chase it. We choose. Accurate and comprehensive contacts are the core of what becomes workable. What we get from this investment is the capability to put effectiveness into operation. Email communications have profound impacts on our innovations and their potency and value are there for our choosing. It is the integrated relationship between calendar, contact, and email that benefits us most when these three roots of operating are fed, firm, and managed.

CHAPTER 2

The Art and Psychology of Scheduling Meetings

There's no better time than now to step back and look at the success of scheduling meetings from a relationship vantage point rather than approach it as disconnected from our many associations. There are several survey creator, poll, and online scheduling software programs available that do work and are useful. Although I have been the receiver of those scheduling approaches, I prefer the benefits of intercommunication synergy. Having the awareness and patience to invest in our relationships will ease the angst of accomplishing the scheduling coordination task. For me, interpersonal communication is more fun, and it fosters collaboration, which increases chances for scheduling availability because a reciprocal desire to be of help is most gratifying. This dyadic communication also breaks down boundaries and builds more lucrative networks. We end up with Team Assistants. If you ever want to witness the possibilities from an ultimate and personal team-based charge, watch *Miracle on Ice*, the men's Olympic 1980 ice hockey medal-round game. It was played in Lake Placid, New York, between the hosting United States and the four-time defending gold medalists, the Soviet Union. It is amazing what can happen when people work together as a team and one plus one equals eleven, and not two. The charge heightens the chance for success, and it fuels the fire.

We Assistants are on the same ship. If anyone can relate to our need to schedule a complex meeting, it is ... indeed ... us. Potential meeting complications include number of attendees, demographic differences, swamped schedules, varying levels of and options for communication technology, and yes, different personalities on different trips. Good news. The common denominator is communal. We and the meeting attendees all want the same thing. Clarity, presence, an agenda, and progress.

Depending on the business we are in, tracking attendance takes on different meanings and therefore warrants different methods. Tracking can occur by website, swipe card reader, self-check-in, code reader, mobile app, etc. There are times we record member attendance and times we want members to sign themselves in manually or by barcode. There are wall mounted time clocks and many attendance tracking software products available. The Assistant has a broader task ahead when it comes to meeting attendance. We are charged with accomplishing the goal of getting the requested attendees (ideally all) together (phone, in person, videoconference, WebEx, combination of the options, etc.), on the same day and at the same time. This may sound easier than it can prove to be.

For those of us who opt out of the exclusive robotic/electronic type of scheduling approach, the following suggestions may help.

Tracking attendance for active meetings can prove fundamental. Printing out our attendance request email that we sent to invited participants is useful because it already notes the meeting title and date/time options. Our active meeting file is best positioned on our desk where the first violin sits in close range to the conductor in an orchestra. As responses come in, jot them on the email cover page because again, all needed information is already on it. I draw a quick grid. Players on the "y" axis, date/time options on the "x" axis (but at the top).

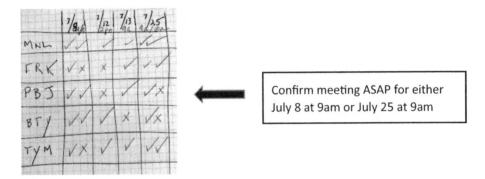

Confirm meeting ASAP for either July 8 at 9am or July 25 at 9am

Check marks, x marks, it soon becomes clear which option will fly or at minimum, it will note the unavailable, whom will get a call from us to negotiate or work out a contingency plan for a meeting results debriefing. Our phone call also allows the unavailable to submit input prior to the meeting. Optimize. Cover these bases because each intended participant is on the invite list for a deliberate reason. "Oh well, sorry you can't make it", is not enough unless it is followed up with a plan that offers the unavailable an opportunity for both contribution and follow up. So, keep it whole. Much more to come on effective communication later.

Back to scheduling, start with the basics and know these: the topic; how soon the meeting is needed; expected length of meeting duration; what are the participation options (in person, phone, videoconference, WebEx, combination of or all of the above); who is mandatory or optional; and fine . . . does it include food/beverage. Go figure - gotta laugh. There are some who need to know that their lunch is coming! I reckon I am one of them. Although this all may seem obvious, how many times have we *not* had one piece of this initial information at the onset, and have had to wait (not just minutes but easily another day or more) or interrupt to get it (not fun . . . at all). Yup. We have all been there. Granted, not the biggest deal, but try being on a great meeting coordination momentum and having a showstopper because we don't know if an extra 30 minutes is expected or if attendance of a certain person is required. While we wait on these seemingly minor details, others' schedules change. We are not only back to step one, we are actually on the negative side of the integer line because we have some re-visiting to do to undo the rest of what we started. Null and void meeting occurrence attempt. Ouch. Another scenario may be that we end up having to take extra steps (extra time) to coordinate yet another meeting for someone who had to leave the meeting early because the meeting duration assumption was one hour and not the needed two. Meeting changes certainly happen that are out of our control. So, minimizing or omitting components that are in our control are well worth our investment. Obtaining all information at the onset leads to a smoother sail.

Confirming meetings can be a sticky wicket. If we do it all the time, we are enabling an expectation and attendees will rely on us for reminders. Assistants optimize when they add both time and progress to their day and not subtract from it. There are occasions to confirm and remind. Yes, we can do this by updating a shared calendar entry, which is useful. Consider there are times to not live only in robot-land and choose to hear the realness and connection in the human exchange. Trust that you will know when the time is beneficial to confirm a meeting. Tap into intuition (Latin *intueri* meaning *consider*). Decisions can become clear when we take the time to consider.

I have to laugh. Hey, credit due to bosses who communicate so effectively with each other. You leaders are movers and shakers – bottom line. Assistants' successes can shine bright through your accomplishments. That being said, your efforts to coordinate your meetings are often highly unsuccessful, albeit your attempts are certainly well intended. Thankfully, alert Assistants are great at interceptions. We know the sooner we catch the ball, the sooner everyone will be where they need to be with materials available. Ball caught. We run to the goal and score. You're welcome and please, leave meeting coordination to the experts. Thank you.

Meeting Coordination through Outlook Invites

OK-OK-OK. Outlook Invites are AMAZING but . . . they can trespass! *Trespass* in Middle English is from Old French meaning *pass over*. One thing an effective Assistant does not like is to be passed over. Case in point. We are at our desk involved with working our day. Enter like a magician's rabbit out of a hat, an unknown calendar Invite. Pops up like a darn Jack-in-the-Box. Boom, a myriad of questions and reactions are in our laps that threaten. Is my boss just being copied on this meeting Invite as a courtesy? Is attendance mandatory or optional? Am I being FYI'd? Why don't I have a heads-up to this? There is a conflict that is not in my control. Will these Invites recur? Who are you anyway?? You've got to be kidding. Assistant, it's time to . . . time-it-out. Take charge in this. Pick up the phone, dial-up the sender, exchange pleasantries and get the needed information. Make the point that we need to make, which is, moving forward, please have the courtesy to check in with us first before assuming it is ok to hit send on your Invite. This way, a connection is made, an understanding is established, and everyone is crystalline clear.

Pause . . . think. OK. Let's consider that there are always departures to every generalization. As much as these pop-up Invites can irk us, let's contemplate a deviation from the above-described brazen act of sending out unsolicited Outlook Invites. It was a friend/colleague who finally convinced me that sending a presumptuous pop-up Invite can actually occupy a niche. Her point and example were testimony to the fact that although beginners know the rules, veterans do know the exceptions. Here it is.

A meeting needs to be scheduled with eight participants and go figure, these players swim in the fishbowl known as most challenging schedules to coordinate, aka uh-oh. The meeting needs to occur within the early part of the following week and boom . . . it is already Thursday afternoon. This meeting coordination effort runs a high risk of unlikelihood. OK. Time to work with what we do know. The participants have advanced notice that this meeting will be taking place and they all have a direct stake in its agenda. This information will help us. Time pressure is on for the Assistant. It would be helpful if we could rely on the schedule settings in Outlook to determine attendance, but meeting participants are not always from within our organizations. Even if they are, it can be difficult to know their verified availability while viewing a purported block time. Enter the benefits of human communication that can turn what is good into what is great. We know the probability of early morning availability is somewhat promising because we know the players. We determine who is an *absolute must attend* and we place a call, maybe two, to our counterparts that we already have an established rapport with (because we have history of shared missions and therefore understanding and respect) to confirm availability for the *absolute must attends*. We then send out the unsolicited Outlook Invite to all. Let it fly and see how the cookie may not crumble! Smart, thoughtful move; a calculated risk worth taking only because in this particular instance, time pressures forced the scheduling approach and degrees of knowledge had been considered. If we are on the receiving end of this type of unsolicited Invite occurrence and we are aware of some of its circumstance, accepting the Invite without questioning it shows understanding and comradery with our counterparts. The word *reciprocity* comes to mind. It is Latin in origin and is defined as *moving backward*

22

and forward. There is something very productive about having reciprocity in our relationships.

Let's swing the pendulum back the other way. We are in mid-workday focused on our computer screen. Pop goes the weasel. We do not recognize anything about the Invite. Suspicion arises because it looks, smells and tastes like a general vendor marketing move. Sorry person! Cheap attempt for you to get your foot in the door. Keep it simple and efficient. Here's how. Delete. Done. If by some slight chance we were incorrect, we can be sure the phone will ring, and we can confirm validity and establish good communication. I highly doubt we were incorrect. All hail the Assistant!

User be grateful for the Outlook Invite way of scheduling meetings for there are so many straight lines to be had. In addition, beware too for some wrinkles that will hopefully be ironed out with starch sometime soon. Following are some examples of potential Invite complications.

A meeting coordination effort is underway, and we are the conductors. *Conductor* via Old French is from *conducere* (Latin) meaning *bring together*. And that is what we do. OK. We have charge of the passengers and are ready to collect the fares. All Aboard! Some are joining the meeting by conference call. We add location directions and agenda attachments to the Outlook Invite (favorable one-stop shopping indeed). We add the dial-in information but hold back on the leader code since that is just meant for our boss. Send . . . sent. Almost a 3-point field goal swish in basketball save the fact that we need to add the leader code *only* to our boss's calendar. This is rather pointless to do because when we attempt to add and then keep the leader code information, the Outlook Invite also sends the information to all invitees. Abort mission. For a short period of time I thought I found a way to circumvent this glitch. When I hit *file* and then *save*, as opposed to *update Invite*, it seemed to work. It saved the leader code to just my calendar. This approach turned out to be a temporary fix and is risky business because, down the line, we may have a meeting time or location change and therefore, need to *update* our Invite. Participants will get the time or location change, but they will also get everything we added since sending the original Invite, like the leader code that what was just meant for our boss. It also doesn't work if we add something and are not the original sender of the Invite. So, it is not a good idea to do the *file/save* approach to record information specific to our boss. What does work, although not ideal, is to make a *boss-only* entry in the calendar separate from, but alongside the meeting Invite on the calendar. This way, no one can screw with it and it is safeguarded.

Another Outlook Invite glitch that I recently experienced happened when I received a meeting Invite whereby my boss would be participating by phone. I added the dial-in information to the notes section in the Invite since it was not provided by the sender. File save. File close. A few days later the sender of the Invite changed the meeting time and updated the Invite. Poof! Another disappearing act. The dial-in information that I added? Gone. It was a 7:30am meeting that he missed. I'm hopeful Invites will soon allow for some tailoring but for now I highlight what I need my boss to know on the top right corner of the back-up material. If there is no back-up, enter the forever-trusted post-it note stuck to her/his phone.

Enter another Invite wrinkle. We've coordinated a meeting that now needs to be cancelled. It was a crucial public hearing that would determine the existence of a needed urgent care center. It would be rescheduled. We send out the Outlook cancellation notice. Poof. That meeting disappears from our calendars. Gone. Dissolved like a water-soluble vitamin. It is no longer on our calendars, yet it remains on others' calendars as *cancelled*. Five weeks pass and it

24

is imperative that our boss knows the original date of the hearing because it affects a time-specific new deadline. Yes. There are time-consuming ways for us to figure out the original date but if Outlook cancellations did not vanish on the sender's calendar like they do, the meeting would still be noted on the original date with the automatic *cancelled* notation preceding it. A quick search would then get us that date. We do have the option to manually re-enter the meeting subject title with note that we cancelled it on our calendars but then why have the *cancel meeting* feature?? While it does work for the recipients' calendars it surprisingly does not work for our calendars.

I recently happened upon another Outlook Invite snafu. An Assistant sent out an Invite to a group of seven. One invitee forwarded the Invite to another person whom she though should be invited. She was likely correct that this person should be included. That is not the point. The Invite maintained the original sender's email address so that all responses went back to the sender and not to the person who had forwarded it. It appeared though, that the forwarded Invite came from the sender when in fact, it did not. This was where the confusion started. Now I don't know if this is related but somehow in the process, the invitee became *owner* of the Invite. Who was getting what at that point was difficult to determine. Please, please, please, desires to add additional people to a meeting should first be addressed directly with the organizer of the meeting. The Assistant can then confirm approval and add the person. I checked in with some Information Technology colleagues on this and general consensus was summed up this way. "It's a strange but normal behavior when forwarding a meeting Invite."

All that being said about Outlook's blunders, it's hard for me to tap into the meeting coordination process pre-Outlook Invite. It is quite phenomenal how this tool grasps the many facets of scheduling and like an eight-inch firework bomb in a mortar – blows it up and out for all to share. Moreover, it allows for general changes through time. Quite astounding.

For a percent of you who may be reading this, the Microsoft Outlook references noted in this book may seem abundant and even outdated. We certainly live in a technical world where once something hits the information highway, we can soon call it dated and at another point obsolete. According to *TechRepublic* (November 7, 2017), 83 percent of enterprises use a version of Microsoft Office in their businesses. The Outlook user percentage is trending downward. If you utilize other software for meeting scheduling, I hope it includes some form of real-time human to human communication. Why? Because it offers something technology cannot. Relationships. Goodness. Respect. Laughter. Connection. Fulfillment.

It works for some meetings to be entered manually and not by Outlook Invite. Entering meetings manually is one's prerogative. If the coordinating person says to us by phone or email, "Just put it in, I'm not sending an Outlook Invite", be-fine-with-that. That person has their reasons and what works for them, will also work for us. I've had people literally insist that I send out an Invite for a meeting that I am coordinating. What that person is thinking remains a mystery to me. I want to be known as that person who will work in whatever way works for a colleague-in-action and for the good of the whole. Here is the caveat. Your show, your right to direct. My show, my right. Respect.

The Art and Psychology of Scheduling Meetings Wrap-Up

An Assistant was super motivated one Monday morning because she had scheduled vacation days for that Thursday and Friday. The Assistant's need for her two days off was not negotiable.

Preparation where possible had begun the prior week so all was in order for her Monday/Tuesday/Wednesday work plan. Hopefully nothing time-consuming and pressing would unexpectedly come her way. Well, it did, and it was unnerving. It felt nearly impossible. Truly. It was a meeting scheduling nightmare request. Here is what happened.

A lot of important work was going on in Administration but as we all know, that is not unusual. It was sometime in the latter half of that Monday morning when the boss hung up the phone and called in the Assistant. He briefed her on the assignment, which was to coordinate team interviews with four people from a strategic planning firm that would be onsite the following week Tuesday at 3:00pm and who would depart that week Friday at Noon. That meant two full days and almost two half days of interviews to schedule. At this point all seemed manageable.

The boss and Assistant drafted up team names and noted participants. After a lot of back and forth, there were – kid you not – 34 teams, each team having anywhere from two to twelve participants. That left 148 people to coordinate. There were duplications of people on various teams, but regardless of that, it stood for additional meeting coordination efforts. After the Assistant's inward reaction of something that fell between tears and exasperation, she decided there was only one way to go about this. The Assistant first typed up the team list and entered each participant's name under yellow-highlighted team titles. To begin with, high clarity and organization were necessary if this would be pulled off. Next, she assigned a lead person from each team by inserting an asterisk by that name.

27

ORGANIZATION LOGO

Revision [Date] - [Company] Interviews ([Days/Dates]

(Team Lead = *; A = [Name of Conference Room; B = [Name of Conference Room]

Team 1 (A)	Team 7 (A)	Team 12 (A)
Team Title	Team Title	Team Title
Name*	Name*	Name*
Name	Name	Name
Name	Name	Name
Name	Name	Name
	Name	
Team 2 (B)	Name	Team 13 (B)
Team Title		Team Title
Name*	Team 8 (B)	Name*
Name	Team Title	Name
	Name*	
	Name	Team 14 (B)
Team 3 (A)	Name	Team Title
Team Title	Name	Name*
Name*		Name
Name	Team 9 (B)	Name
Name	Team Title	
	Name*	
Team 4 (A)	Name	Team 15 (B)
Team Title	Name	Team Title
Name*		Name*
Name	Team 10 (B)	Name
Name	Team Title	
Name	Name*	Team 16 (A)
	Name	Team Title
Team 5 (B)	Name	Name*
Team Title	Name	Name
Name*	Name	Name
Name		Name
Name	Team 11 (B)	
Team 6 (A)	Team Title	Team 17 (A)
Team Title	Name*	Team Title
Name*	Name	Name*
Name	Name	Name
Name		Name
Name		Name

Etc.

Then she created a table in Word that included day/hour timeslots, team name, and two columns defining the conference room locations since there would be two interview sessions occurring simultaneously. She bartered fairly to get two conference rooms in close proximity to each other.

28

ORGANIZATION LOGO

[Company] Interview Schedule
[Days/Dates]
Revision [Date]

Date	Interview A-[Conf Rm Name]	Interview B-[Conf Rm Name]
Tuesday, July 10	**Team**	**Team**
3:00pm	13 - Team Title	26 - Team Title
4:00pm	32 - Team Title	5 - Team Title
5:00pm	30 - Team Title	
Wednesday, July 11		
8:00am	7 - Team Title	10 - Team Title
9:00am		
10:00am	4 - Team Title	
11:00am	6 - Team Title	[Individual Mtg]
12 Noon	27 - Team Title	21 - Team Title
1:00pm	22 - Team Title	24 - Team Title
2:00pm	3 - Team Title	2 - Team Title
3:00pm	12 - Team Title	11 - Team Title
4:00pm	16 - Team Title	
Thursday, July 12		
8:00am	17 - Team Title	8 - Team Title
9:00am	35 - Team Title	15 - Team Title
10:00am	33 - Team Title	25 - Team Title
11:00am		14 - Team Title
12 Noon	20 - Team Title	[Individual Mtg]
1:00pm	29 - Team Title	
2:00pm	19 - Team Title	9 - Team Title
3:00pm	TOUR w/ [Name]	
4:00pm	31 - Team Title	
Friday, July 13		
8:00am	1 - Team Title	[name]
9:00am	28 - Team Title	[name]
10:00am	18 - Team Title	[name]
11:00am	34 - Team Title	[name]
Reschedule: [name]; [name]; [name]; [name]		

Conference Rooms: A - [Conf Rm Name] / B - [Conf Rm Name]

She then drafted an email and sent it to the team leads that explained the purpose for the interviews and requested that they coordinate with the members of their team and email back three day and time slot options in preference order. She attached the schedule to the email. Replies came in like wildfire because when people know they count and are asked to be heard, they show up to the party. At that point, the Assistant began to fill in the schedule and the mission was accomplished throughout the next two days. She then sent out the confirmation Invites. She had her Thursday/ Friday off free of worry. She anticipated, she prepped, and she took care of the job and herself.

OK. # 1. This monster of meeting coordination in a short time frame IS possible. What it took was: a choice made to have a *can-do* perspective, planning, organization, and a sense of humor. Just as important, if not more, is . . . # 2. There's no better time than now to step back and look at the success of scheduling meetings from a relationship vantage point rather than to approach it as disconnected from our many associations. It's the relationships that we nourish that increase the metabolism of a successful effort.

In hindsight, this Assistant did have an option whereby the team leads could have entered their time slot preference directly on a shared collaborative document. Perhaps this approach would have saved a bit of time, although it would have lacked needed vim and vigor. Throughout the process, it was the communication and juggling from the Assistant that ignited the effort. The infusion of teamwork in live time added to a sense of excitement and a desire for inclusion. Happy people are more driven, willing, and inspired. Results result.

CHAPTER 3
Assistant to Assistant Relationships

So, where do we get the *charge* that we need to continue our mission to be optimized? In Latin, *optimus* means *best* and early 19th century English adds the *–ize*, giving us optimize. OK. *Best* does make sense. I imagine we all agree that we work toward optimization by investing in all parts of ourselves. It was interesting to discover that the word origin for *invest* in Latin means *in-* (*into, upon*) and *vestire* (*clothe*). OK. *In-clothe* makes not-so-much sense. A further look into the word *invest* notes *clothe with the insignia of a rank* and *endow with authority*. This implies progressive movement toward advancement. No matter how it is cut, optimizing and investing greatly rely on each other. A sustainable charge needs something more valuable than the quick fix caffeine jolt to get our wheels in sustainable motion. Aside from the self-work we all hopefully practice, good energy from others is a sure bet if we are looking to ignite. Alternatively, if we are looking to deflate, find the bad energy! It will work all the time. Invest to optimize.

When I threw my thoughts about Assistant relationships into the washing machine, this is what went into the dryer: Good Energy;

Happiness; Respect; Bad Energy; Rectification; Sensitivity; and, Synergy. Here we go.

Good Energy. For many years, phone meetings between my boss and a political economist have been coordinated by me and Shawn, the economist's Assistant. It is a simple, 30-minute monthly call that is set up by Outlook Invite. When the day or time needs to change, Shawn and I have a brief phone call - bing, bang, boom - Outlook Invite update occurs. At one point, unbeknownst to me, Shawn was promoted, and I now coordinate the meeting changes with Raina. Coordination remains straightforward. One day I dialed up Raina who apparently had a day off and Shawn surprisingly picked up the phone. It had been at least a year since our last collaboration. Charge! I really don't know anything at all about Shawn, but we coordinated the meeting change with a super-upbeat familiarity. My day's momentum stayed on track and an extra charge was added to it. It is so very great to work with the *Shawns* of the world who we don't even really know! There is so much power to be found when shared missions are exercised with simple precision and happiness.

Happiness. A six-year old stayed up late one night so that she could watch the opening ceremony of the Olympic Games. She loved the costumes, dancers, and drums. The camera panned to a speed-skater contender a number of times capturing her enthusiasm and larger than life smiles and laughter. Every time that occurred, the little girl would start to giggle and broke out laughing. Her dad asked her what was so funny, and the little girl threw up her arms and in utter delight exclaimed, "I don't know! That lady just makes me so happy!" That right there is unadulterated happiness. It's both compelling and infectious. Just imagine for a moment what it would be like to work with only happy people.

Respect. Our Assistant relationships with each other, both within and outside our organizations, require hardcore respect.

32

Respect is Latin in origin, *respicere*, and means *look back at*. Thoughtful observation free of judgement and full of trust comes to mind.

Let me tell you about Jenna, an Executive Assistant and my counterpart at an alike organization. Unfortunately, it was the deeply-rooted-in-plentiful-history type of organizational rival with a lot at stake for both camps. It was just not going to happen. Leadership motives resided on opposite poles. The wolf did not live with the lamb and the leopard did not lie down with the goat. The State mandated an affiliation between the two organizations and for about three long years, the futile attempt was made to swim in the same stream. Tensions dictated deliberate and carefully calculated moves. Assistants, although not in the fire, certainly feel intense heat, so Jenna and I walked the tightrope, performing feats of balance. Jenna is a cool, classy, intelligent, and funny person. We clicked so well that we entertained the idea of meeting for dinner one night. Perceptions (being what we all know them to be) caused us brief pause when considering our social get-together but truth in motive is indeed liberating and dinner plans proceeded. Hopefully your bosses are like mine who appreciated the notice, only because he understood perceptions as well. He simply said, "have a great time" and meant it. Jenna and I had many dinners over the years where we spoke about movies, life, shared pictures, and laughed our heads off. Our work lives remained both unexpressed and sacred. What we shared regarding work was a deep and unspoken understanding. As expected, nothing newsworthy came from these dinner meetings. Oh wait. One thing did. We discovered the spot for the best fish tacos ever. Respect. Regard. Reverence.

More on Respect. It is good practice to treat other Assistants the same way that we want to be treated. An important call was needed by a Chief Financial Officer (CFO) that had to take place as soon as possible regarding the financing of a business venture. ASAP really meant ASAN (Now). Email correspondence was sent from one Assistant to the other, who responded on her boss's availability. In the meantime, one CFO called the other CFO for whatever reason and apparently, a 2:30pm call-time was determined between the two of them. One Assistant, by chance, was in close enough proximity to be able hear what had transpired. It is only by that chance that the Assistant knew that no further effort was needed. If all were perfect, the new status would have been communicated but intense work can occupy the mind, and Assistants can suffer the ramifications of suddenly being out of the loop. We owe it to each other to include each other. If we get emails and we notice an Assistant is not included, let's make it our business to forward it right over. Let's communicate a closure or a status that we may know of when the other Assistant does not. We have a great opportunity in our role to be pivotal in nurturing unification business wide. It's a responsibility that we can be grateful for. Let's be sure to practice it with each other too. We all know how it feels when we are firing on all cylinders. It's quite a rush. Let's share in it.

Bad Energy. What proves difficult are the Assistant to Assistant relationships that are soured. Most challenging are Assistants within the same organization who must work closely together. I know a lawyer who has two Assistants who split up the workweek. For the most part, they have the same job responsibilities for the same boss. Their relationship is competitive and mimics slight-of-hand moves in card magic. I cannot imagine having that day-in and day-out existence. Their relationship affects more than just them. Simple deduction dictates that it actually affects other people and business as well. Survivable – yes. Productivity – stunted. If these two Assistants were in therapy together, they would have the same choice all relationships have: decide to work it out or go your separate ways. After an impressive sixteen years of this co-existence, likely only due to the need for employment and health insurance benefits, the relationship actually ended due to one Assistant's retirement. Wowza.

34

An Assistant's negative behavior holds a power that can threaten and influence the office atmosphere. The following faux pas (French meaning embarrassing or tactless act or remark in a social situation) thankfully taught me an important lesson. Many years ago, pre-healthcare, I was a baker. I had some conflicts with leadership that if I remember correctly, began with my quest to determine and quantify donut waste. Sounds so funny to me now, but not-at-all-funny tensions grew. A new employee began work one day and I was asked to train this person. I did. When I cautioned the employee about my opinion of high-maintenance leadership (ooops), I got shut down. She point-blank told me to cease and desist – that relationships have the right to be determined by each person. Thank you, Ms. I-Wish-I-Remembered-Your-Name. Your directness with me to set me straight was taken on the chin and a valuable lesson was learned, very much appreciated, and never forgotten. Why choose to infiltrate negative energy into the work environment when we can do the opposite and have a favorable effect.

More on Bad Energy. I know an Assistant who is responsible for thirteen people in a large organization and in her role(s) she needs to consistently communicate and coordinate with other Assistants. Although a good number of them are sensitive and supportive of her circumstance, there are a few, and yes, one in particular, who poses as a barricade every time the Assistant tries to improve her situation. The point is, there are many of us who have it very rough and could use encouragement and assistance from our peers. If we are not a team creating progress, then our organization loses, and we lose. Shame on those who choose to close a door on someone when they can opt to open it.

Rectification. Life is not so ideal that we can keep company with only those that we are at ease with. Going to work can become so burdensome when we know we are heading into pre-determined psyche-clash. Sails are useless with no wind and the quest for relationship connection and optimization stands little chance when this dynamic is present. There are times when putting effort into relationship improvement is the very last thing we want or are willing to do. But we all must survive our day, so we try the angles . . . ignore, judge, gossip, set up a force-field around us, be distressed, pretend we are not bothered, or draw presumptuous conclusions. What we are left with is our unhappy and unfulfilled selves and some thick air.

· If you are currently in this seemingly doomed dynamic, rest easy. First off: "meQtaHbogh qachDaq Suv qoH neH". For those of you who are not Star Trek fans, that's Klingon for "Only a fool fights in a house that continues to burn." If you want to get out of the burning house, decide on change or give up if you denounce the possibility of solution. *Change* by the way, is Celtic in origin and in Latin is *cambiare* meaning *barter*. Meet yourself at the big oak table and come to terms with change on the horizon, even if you do not know what that will look like. This phase of rectification is essential. Next, choose patience, not with your situation, or with the other person – but with you. Patience, from Latin *patientia* means *endurance, submission*. Look. If the game is over the gear comes off. Erase the chalkboard (or Smartboard for you millennials) regardless of your lurking sentiments about someone else. To step forward, we must face ourselves. What can outperform what we are in the habit of thinking is the ability to alter our thoughts to new views. This is in our control. Willingness. Patience. Contemplation. Perception. I once made the mistake of thinking that the problem was a person. When I worked on changing my patterns of thinking, it turned out the problem I was foundationally having was the process and not the person. Even if we are convinced that the problem is the person, our focus is misdirected. Draining. Negative. Pointless. Time and heart draining. Before I fully realized that my perceptions were in my control, I learned the lesson the hard way. My boss's solution to his lead astray Assistant was to refocus my attention by giving me two new major projects. Good move on his part, ouch on my part. Now I know to pivot my submarine periscope toward the work at hand and not toward others.

"If you are willing to look at another person's behavior toward you as a reflection of the state of their relationship with themselves rather than a statement about your value as a person, then you will, over a period of time cease to react at all."
-Yogi Bhajan

So how do we see things differently, especially when our judgements can inhabit the earth's inner core? Take the idea of *six degrees of separation*. It suggests that all living things and everything else in the world are six or fewer steps away from each other. I once had a physician friend of mine explain in detail what that meant. It all sounded amazingly phenomenal, but I remained a bit blank. So, I decided that to me, *six degrees of separation* means waaaaay too close at times. And that is how come we can get stuck at an impasse with our relationships. Gaining some space can tilt the scale from the emotion to the intellect where we can observe our own situations more clearly because we can quiet our minds.

More on Self-observation. Many years ago, I spoke with my sister Amy about a work relationship conflict that I was having. I don't remember any of the specifics, but I do remember my issue was affecting me terribly. She recommended that I put myself in an observer role in my own situation. She told me to step out and take a look at it from the outside in and to view it with peculiar interest. My oh my, objectivity at work and a chance for some fog to clear. Space. Considering options is easier when we de-personalize. Back up. Back way the heck up. Sometimes we are so close to something that we feel epoxied there, unable to see that we actually can choose to move. Consider the Dionaea Muscipula (aka Venus flytrap) as an example of entrapment. It has lobes that exhibit rapid plant movement by snapping shut in about 0.1 seconds when special sensory hairs are stimulated. When the lobes are continuously stimulated, the edges of the lobes grow or fuse together, sealing the trap and creating an enclosed "stomach" in which digestion and absorption can take place. In tense situations let's not let ourselves be eaten by the Venus flytrap. It is wise to stand back from being too close. It's crazy how many people choose discord over using the basic *observer role* approach to conflict resolution.

What can we do when stuck? We can take the time to realize that all people share personal situations of private struggles. So, right there we have something in common with our adversarial colleagues. We can calm ourselves; we can expand cognitive space and can redirect our attention. We can find things that mean more in our work situations than the contentious conclusions that our thoughts have drawn. After all, they are only thoughts. Sounds simpler than it feels? Maybe consider that it is not as complicated as we might have thought. The motive? Well, after all, who doesn't want to be content?

Sensitivity. Although Assistant interactions usually begin with one person's needs and then collaboration is quickly established, there are great opportunities regarding our sensitivities to each other. Sensory, as in, *to perceive/to feel*, is where meaningful and worthwhile human connections become realized. Following are two examples that typify sensitivity.

Ann called from another organization. Immediately, I could hear between the lines. She did not complain at all. She didn't have to. I understood. My colleague's plate was full, and cup was topped off. Rescue underway and all it took was the offer to contact 50% of her meeting's attendees. Her relief was the only thank you needed.

One time an Assistant apologized to me for forgetting to include a copy of an important lease that was needed for a meeting. The email apology did not come in written words. Instead it came in an image of the cutest-ever puppy dog with the big, round, sad eyes. It made me smile. Assistant communication exchanges can be hysterical, kind, and supportive. It is nothing short of admirable how they manage to maintain professional focus and progress while being thoughtful and warmhearted.

Synergy. Assistants as a group are a force right there backing up the leaders of our organizations. No small potatoes in our field! Adding effort to our shared relationships with each other can propel our desired outcomes, make us even stronger, and will prove to be worth the investment. At times when being overwhelmed threatens, it is often the interactions we have with each other that can bring us back to home base. This synergy can also push us forward. Here is a case in point regarding the power of synergy.

A young man was in training for his first ever marathon. He trained according to plan, but the twenty-six miles ahead had a foundational unknown, like, how was this going to play out. *Take your mark!* was called and off he went. Although there were both neutral and euphoric times throughout the run, he also experienced phases that reflected stages of grief and loss but in reverse. The run began with acceptance and after some time, hit emotions of lurking despair, many miles of bargaining, and some anger points to try to motivate. He skipped over the denial phase since there was no denying the course he was on. Up came mile eighteen, which was a struggle because although much had been accomplished, the eight miles ahead were a hefty chunk of questionable change. As he was mindfully trying to pull a rabbit out of a hat, he sensed a fellow racer behind him to his left. The runner steadily passed him, patted him on the shoulder, gave a quick nod and said, "You got this." And off he trotted. This pay-in-kind act is just what the young rookie needed. As he raised his head with some newfound motivation, his view of the friendly and supportive racer included a yellow shirt, black running shorts and a prosthetic limb. Goes without saying but saying it anyway, he finished those eight miles without a doubt in mind. *Synergy* is Greek in origin, *sun* (together) and *ergon* (work), giving us *sunergos* (working together). Yes. Synergy can push us forward.

More on Synergy. There was email communication with Amelia regarding a meeting coordination. The meeting time moved to 12:30pm so Amelia was now determining lunch. She inquired about sandwich preference for the attendees. I responded, "anything just no onions for one of the participants". She stepped it up and sent specific available menu options. Go girl. I responded with the more-detailed order. She thanked me and added her desire for tiramisu. She did not know that at that point in time I was sitting in a pile of excessiveness. There was too much air in my balloon. Despite that, her comment made me smile. I thanked her. I got a reply. It was an image of a double-scoop chocolate ice cream with caramel sauce and it said, "For You Heidi". Togetherness. Synergy.

40

Assistant to Assistant Relationships Wrap-Up

There are two concurrent halves that operate with Assistants. One is what we are managing ourselves and the other is what we are managing with each other. 50/50 - interesting ratio to think about. The days of working in silos are indeed over. Years ago, there was a sense that our value could be gauged by being the only one who knew so much about our responsibilities. There was a perception that job security was increased by choosing this isolated approach. Meanwhile interdepartmental turf wars were what increased. *It's not in my job description!* Time warp ahead. Worth and progress are now visible when the mindset is shared, and organizational barriers are broken down. Go the way of fusion.

Meaningful and productive Assistant relationships do not happen by chance. By doing for each other, we both give and get. It adds substance to quality and allows for relationship evolvement. I experience it every day with so many of you. You bring joy to work.

CHAPTER 4
Minutes

Just a few but important *Taking Minutes* items to address, the first of which is the acknowledgement that Minutes is most certainly a major misnomer. It would more appropriately be called *Forever Interrupted Hours.*

Now that we have that shared opinion out of the way, let's find the beauty in this prize of a responsibility. But first, some stratagems to maneuver more reasonably though this important task.

There are generally two basic ways to take Minutes. One is in table format where we see titles like specific report, status, responsible party, and action items. These Minutes are often found in landscape layout. They are direct, action-based, and easy to absorb. The other option is more narrative in nature and offers a more detailed account of current events. Action items and resolutions are in bold font.

The following situation is what led me to choose my style of Minute taking. I began my role in the president's office during record low times for the organization, and sometime in the latter half of the 90's, the organization's viability could not be justified to say the least. There were questions that pertained to operations in landslide as well as the confusion of an audited discrepancy of an estimated $20 to $30 million. Let's just say that temporary transfers can fail miserably. To this day, I am still relieved that after an arduous investigation, the Attorney General found no malfeasance. It didn't change the fact that the staff and board in particular needed to somehow put verifiable meaning to literally every single number in finance moving forward in order to save a relatively large organization - and that would only be a starting point. Financing aside, the heart of the organization was beating slowly. Yes. Those first board meetings were . . . I still cannot find the right words. Perhaps there are not any. I do remember being in awe of board and key management members who faced this situation with only the health of the organization in mind. At that time, I was new to my role as Assistant. I also remember longing for my prior career as a baker, back when my time was consumed with caring for a Nubian goat show herd in northern California. Reality was what it was, and I was scared but proud to stand with the courageous people. For all reasons just noted, I chose the latter option for taking Minutes, which was to record a more detailed account of current events. I figured it was prudent at that point to record more rather than less information. I had the good fortune to have the secretary of the board review my Minutes during that time. Passing Minutes through him was like taking a five-credit college crash course. If you can find or are lucky enough to have this type of mentor, your Minute-taking skills will become accurate and fluid. So Minute style ends up being what makes most sense for the circumstance at hand.

Completing Minutes weighs heavily on the Assistant because of the high degree of focus and importance that are required. Assistants' days are filled with everything imaginable and how we prioritize our days is for us to determine. It is important for us to be able to address our immediate responsibilities while at the same time be on top of what is due as well as what has not yet occurred. Minutes is an item that can easily be put off because busy weeks can go by and there is not a time slot for the direct attention that Minutes require. Capital A Plus for our efforts when we finally return to our Minutes and all we have written is literally the first half of a sentence and that was over a week ago! That is not an exaggeration. I know a number of us who have, on too many occasions, found ourselves staying late or being at home whipping out these puppies because time did run out. The good practice to avoid this scenario begins with a concrete decision that we make early on, as in, soon after the meeting has occurred. The decision will say something like, "Self. . . I have a volunteer this coming Tuesday morning for three hours and my firm priority is my Minutes", or something similar. If you do not utilize volunteers, choose to figure it out. Let's not be victim to our own circumstance. Let it be known to the appropriate parties that we have called this play. It will be a morning where we opt to return calls at a later point regardless of if it is not our common practice to do so. We all know there are exceptions to the "do-not-interrupt" approach, but we can drastically minimize roadblocks when we set design our own show. The relief of Minute closure is well worth our investment. Concrete decision. Commit.

Commitment established. Following are three suggestions that will help to streamline the Minutes effort. There is actually a fourth suggestion that I will start with and one that I have used an unadmitted amount of times. Here it is. If you are listening to the meeting digitally/audibly while typing your Minutes, increase the sound rate lever until you can sit back and enjoy listening to the meeting participates, aka *Alvin and the Chipmunks*. It is hysterical.

Suggestion A. If we take Minutes for multiple meetings, chances are high that much of the information is the same except it is tailored appropriately for each audience. Within a month's period of time, there can be, let's say, three major meetings: leadership, board, and strategic planning. If these sets of Minutes are sitting on our desks, let's start with the one that will be most comprehensive, regardless of which upcoming meeting will be the first to occur. In other words, if we don't like the peas on our dinner plates, let's eat them first because the rest of the dinner will be more appetizing. We have already decided that we are on offense and that all Minutes will be completed before each meeting with time to spare. OK. Jackhammer to the concrete. First set complete. Work our game plan. As we get to the second and third sets of Minutes, we will already have key paragraphs to cut, paste, and then tweak accordingly. Additionally, this cut/paste/tweak technique works with annual items i.e., term lists, motions, introductions to audit reports, etc., because the wording is the same. We worked hard to get it written correctly the prior year. Waste no time, and perhaps the only change will be something as simple as the day/month/year.

If we happen to just have one set of outstanding Minutes then let's get on it. Our cut/paste/tweak opportunity can then come down the pike.

Suggestion B. There are certain times to pull from the experts, but this option should not become habit. We are actively engaged in our Minutes and are moving along well when we hit a stop sign because sometimes the topic becomes intricate. Although the presenter is well versed, the specifics are complex. Legal jargon abounds and in 60 seconds a myriad of court filing specifics are reported. We feel like Bobblehead action and toy figures on the dashboard of someone else's car. In this type of instance, we can script an email to the expert acknowledging her/his proficiency and delivery and ask for the courtesy of a short summary paragraph. She/he likely owes us a few favors anyway, and if this option is not overused, a perfectly willing response will come. Reciprocity at work.

Suggestion C. Similar to Suggestion B but with less effort is our option to utilize our *best-friend-forever* to access needed factual information. Search engine use is an invention benchmark that has catapulted our ability to retrieve information. It is so phenomenal and has had such a life-changing impact that it can sometimes feel like it has always existed. Use it for those cutting-edge, reported items that are already well written and on-point. Assistants consistently get a gift. We get a continual education while at work (reference Chapter 10, *The Assistant/Boss Relationship* for more on this point). Use of the search engine can be quite convenient.

Minutes Wrap-Up

Assistants take pride. Consider that Minute-taking is to be revered. What we are putting in print is permanent . . . and it is history worth writing.

CHAPTER 5
Logistics and Streamlining

The origin of the word *logistics* is rooted in 1620's Medieval Latin and meant *pertaining to logic*, which in Greek is *logike*, and meant *word/reason*. In late 19th century French, it meant *lodge, movement and supplying of troops and equipment.*

The word *streamline* dates back to 1868 and meant *line drawn from point to point, so that its direction is everywhere that of the motion of the fluid.* Sometime in 1898, *free from turbulence* was added and then in 1907 there came a sense of *shaped so that the flow around it is smooth.*

This chapter aims to offer a mix of rational workspace recommendations that reasonably flow with the current. Logistics and Streamlining together can furnish us with a high level of proficiency and preparedness.

Logistics

Improving our general office space including our hard copy and computer file systems is a tangible way to escalate our performance.

It is logical to have items available and accessible to us throughout our entire office space. Our thoughts and plans should relate to our physical work environment so that what we organize in our minds reflects our space in an efficient and sensible way. What does this mean? The key we frequently use to open the conference room door should be in that right-there drawer, not across the room in the back of a file cabinet. Our conference room remote controls are placed in the drawer by the videoconference screen. Our supply closets have their own practicality. We work with two computer monitors so that we can view meeting requests, conference room availability, and multiple calendars in one view and can slide/copy all information wherever needed. Our project folders are accessible by the spin of our chair and are in order of priority. There is rationale to where our phones, keyboards, printers, and computer screens are placed. Design and arrange so that safe and easy use is achieved. Ergonomics.

It's here – I know it's here – uhhh – It's here – uhhh – hold on – I know it's here . . .

Some claim to function well in the face of their all-over-the-place piles because they "know where everything is". I have tried to understand this conviction because I do know sufficiently functioning and successful people who operate this way. However, I'm taking a stand on this one. I recently saw Alice Cooper at 70 years old raise his performance to jaw dropping standards. Having been to a number of these shows, I promise you that he and his band never disappoint fans. Great, great times. It's never too late to improve our performance and create newness. Consider these as examples. Bertha Wood had her first book, *Fresh Air and Fun: The Story of a Blackpool Holiday Camp*, published on her 100th birthday in 2005. Charles Darwin was 50 years old when he published *On the Origin of the Species*, the book that supported the theory for which he is best known by. Twelve years after being known as the first astronaut to orbit planet Earth, John Glenn became a US Senator in Ohio, a position he held for 24 years. Anna Mary Robertson Moses (Grandma Moses), was a housekeeper and farm laborer before beginning her painting career at 78 years old. In 2006, one of her paintings sold for $1.2 million. So even greatness can grow. Clean up your desks office people.

More on accessibility. Why it took me so long to establish my *Work Holy Binder* remains a mystery. Assistants get the complete gamut when it comes to the scope and type of questions that we receive. If we don't know the answer, we must know where to get it. For years, I would place calls to the Comptroller for an insurance provider number and to the Foundation department for their tax-exempt number. I would call Human Resources to get employment dates of leadership for grant applications and I would call Quality Management for user codes to access survey results. On and on and on. Finally, noting that a pattern had set in, I created a basic, quick-reference information sheet. It grew through time as other repetitive actions sprouted, i.e., updated board lists; operating certificates; restaurant locations with their seasonal schedule; law firm contact sheets; interpreter language/contact information; local hotel accommodation details; master contact spreadsheets for management; tables of organization; access codes; committee member assignments; fire alarm codes; etc. This binder is now frequently utilized. If there were a handful of items I needed to grab before the building went down in flames, the *Work Holy Binder* would be one of them.

The idea of logical and accessible items ought to carry over from our mind sets and work environments to our computer and hard copy file systems. Simply put, computer management works well when it reflects our mind and physical office synergy. If we could start completely fresh with computer file organization, set-up of this *accessible* factor would be clearer. The ideal situation would be to have years of Assistant experience, begin employment at a brand-new business and have full knowledge and forethought of its strategic plan. We can set up a computer file system from only an understanding and a vision. This is certainly not most of our situations. We begin everywhere but fresh. There is history, someone else's idea of organization and often a fragmented view of a ton of often displaced information. To top it off, businesses are always in some sort of motion and change keeps altering everything. It could take a full-time employee in a babysitter role to manage computer files. Let's say the computer management situation is a mess. It's time to exercise patience and a plan.

"Patience is bitter, but its fruit is sweet."
-Jean-Jacques Rousseau

Leave no gap between intention and action. Know that we can gradually and relentlessly solve disarray by chipping away items one dimension at a time. The organization I am in began in 1909, so it's the Sequoiadendron Giganteum (Giant Redwood tree) to me. Yes, work can feel 164-279 feet high and 20-26 feet in diameter. There is a fine line I need to ride between organizing computer files that are, or are soon to be, somewhat obsolete (and that includes files that will always maintain some degree of importance), and those items that are active, essential, and frequently utilized.

It helps to take some time to think through our computer file set-up. The set-up I currently use, which remains a work in progress, differs greatly from what I used for years. This is due to three reasons.

1) The business has evolved to a new level and identity. 2) Early on I did not anticipate the bigger picture. 3) Software changes are imminent. For example, the transmission of a Word document has tilted to the more favorable and secure PDF document.

Think through. Sometimes it makes sense to house certain documents by year while other times they are best stored by topic, project, person, forms, speeches, templates, announcements, or whatever works for our reality and vision. One universal must is to put our fully executed legal documents in the mother-mansion where *only* the latest and greatest reside. Step way back and view from the mind's eye. Anticipate change. Think big. Think broad. Think forward.

Here is just one of umpteen examples that pertain to the logic behind computer file accessibility. My not-for-profit organization recently merged with a state-run institution. One could only imagine the intricacies and enormity of this type of affiliation. Although the Materials Management department was fully engaged in the new logo branding of all forms, the administrative Assistants also needed their computer documents, i.e. minutes, agendas, flyer, invitations, and itineraries, upgraded to the new logo. There were three styles of the logo to choose from. I saved the options to my computer where it made some sense to be. This *accessible* item took five clicks to find and then place. I also had to think on its home because this was just one of a ridiculous number of items that my brain needed to keep track of. It finally dawned on me to resave the logo file to my desktop so now I can click and drag between my two screens in a nanosecond. OK. Maybe it's not one billionth of a second but it is close. We can sometimes think that we run a streamlined plan, and in so many ways, we do. At times, it's just habit that hides opportunity. We also can overlook the crooked lines because of real pressures. Although the solution to the logo anecdote seems so obvious, chances are high that there are a good number of areas in our work scenes that can use some straighter lines. It's the investment in straightening these lines that will work toward optimization. Like the visual of a wood chopping competition, stick with it and the tree will come down.

Many years ago, I remember hearing about businesses going paperless. Depending on the profession, hard copy files seem either minimal or abundant. The most important hard copy files include those original and fully executed documents that stand up in a court of law, i.e., original permits, resolutions, and agreements.

When we use logic, our decisions are backed up with stable rationale and our entire work environment becomes more aerodynamic.

Streamlining

The answer to the question about *how* we survive our days is up to us. Our days can exist in chaos or in order and can also waffle between the two. There are so many opportunities for us to streamline, perhaps too many, and it is easy to overlook many of them. The act of streamlining simplifies tasks, bypasses unnecessary steps, and cuts waste. Saving time ranks amongst the top-tier benefits of streamlining. By untangling and refining, we create a smooth-running situation for ourselves and others.

Most streamlining opportunities are hands-on tangible. Think. Identify. Act. Other opportunities require conceptual thinking, which is the ability to analyze hypothetical situations to acquire insight. These opportunities are more situational. In this case we think broadly about why something is being done. Then we can apply our new thoughts and adjust to a more streamlined process.

Tangible streamlining. We need to coordinate a meeting with two other Assistants. One alternative is to email them to coordinate the meeting. Then . . . we wait. The coordination becomes an open item for an unknown amount of time. Enter - an opportunity to employ faster and simpler working methods. We dial up one Assistant on the phone. We exchange pleasantries and say that we will be getting the other Assistant on the phone to coordinate the meeting. We hit transfer from the open line and dial the third party. The Assistant picks up and we hit the conference button. All on. No delay of back and forth and no needed step to set up a conference line for the coordination. Party time! In live time the three of us are now together equipped with calendars and we hash it out. Anytime I do this, there is an up-beat shared enthusiasm of closure. Assistants LOVE to not add an outstanding item to their day. Thanks! Ha! Have a great day! Let's hang up before something changes! Ah hahahaha. Waiting for responses on too many items on too many occasions is not an efficient use of our time.

Streamlining can occur right where we sit. Earlier we covered printing out a cover page of an email as reference for meeting logistics, like attendance taking. This labor-saving page can effectually include other meeting logistics, i.e., message left with date, next step with date expectation, and key name and phone number. Cover all basic aspects of meeting coordination on this information sheet so with a quick focus of our eyes we can see *exactly* where the status is and therefore avoid the inefficient investigation phase. Streamline.

Although an Assistant's proactive nature is crucial, streamlining can actually occur by holding back at times. Let's talk about this fine line. We have just returned from a meeting and we peruse through emails that have occurred while we were out. We delete what we can so that we can absorb action items more readily. Action item revealed. An important coordination effort is underway and there are many cooks in the kitchen. Too many quite frankly and they all have a relevant degree of static charge to their input. Good time to sit back and let it play out for a bit. What often happens is that energies heighten so players' frustrations increase and closure for meeting coordination becomes more distant. There is a concise point for the mindful Assistant to interject. Instead of entering this jam-up, at the right time, wrap up the package, be the voice of reason, and be the answer. This is possible because we have let it play out and we can see it, contemplate over it, reel it in, and make it work. This can often be accomplished in a one-shot deal. Plus, we can delete a string of emails having only skimmed them. Only eight words of caution. Let's do our best to not alienate anyone.

Streamlining at times can come with a disguise. There are times when taking an extra step proves more efficient then not doing so. In our hands is a 59-page bylaws document. It has clearly passed through mailings, interoffice envelopes, and too many people. It's not on anyone's computer. It's worn self has physically not withstood the test of time. It needs to be scanned and emailed to a law firm. A million and one things to do and this one we want off our desk and out of our head. We are like Roadrunner outsmarting

  Wile E. Coyote. Beep! Beep! (Although the background artist Paul Julian's preferred spelling of the sound affect was "hmeep hmeep"). If you don't know who these dynamic duo cartoon characters are, Wile E. Coyote is always on the chase to eat the Road Runner. Scan done. Back to computer.

Sent to firm. Next. We move on and then the phone rings or there is an email response. Page 32 is missing. Re-do. Darn. There are times to take the time and take the extra step. Check the page count and if need be, manually count the pages *before* sending. When to pick up speed and when to slow it down calls for a clear head that pays attention to detail while not letting the broader goal fade. With experience and practice we will become adept at gauging this disguised streamlining tool. Yes, we are scanning and sending but really what we are doing is getting a critical and complete document to where it needs to be.

Conceptual streamlining. We streamline the tangible and we also can streamline the way we situate our days. Since emails have opened up communication to cover information-sharing 24/7/365, I have found it a wise priority to address, to varying degrees that I decide, all new emails at the *onset* of the day, post coffee. This is so because we create an entire day of catch-up if we don't. We end up chasing carrots that hopefully get within our reach before mid- or end-day. Too much time can be spent getting to the status if two, three, four hours have passed. Beginning our days on offense puts us in the driver's seat. Ok. What's next. Briefly absorb the calendar day so that at our day's *onset* we freshly begin with knowing what to expect. It's easy to jump into a day not aware of its general plan. When aware, we know the pockets that we will have to focus on for more project-based responsibilities. These pockets usually occur when our boss is occupied. Think through how we schedule boss meetings. Look, know, plan, and go. Streamline.

"In order to improve the mind, we ought less to learn, than to contemplate."
-Rene Descartes

Here is another example of conceptual streamlining. We need three invoices from a hotel in Boston from a prior month. Main reservation desk called – request made – promises made – time passes, and no result. A call back and it becomes apparent that there is growing confusion and agitation. Who knows, maybe it's a new person or perhaps a system glitch. We can wait it out or we can jump and address. Optimized Assistants choose the latter. Get the right person on the phone. There is always someone who can cut to the chase. Connecting with this necessary person is accomplished by staying positive, disarming people who are on defense, and relating. These three practices open channels toward solution. No one wants or needs a problem. Let's get our happy selves to where we need to be and not get caught in or be a part of existing complications. The results of our situations depend on our choice to take the long way where blame and frustration can abound or fly like the crow with a much nicer view. Optimized Assistants are about solutions and equanimity.

Closing out our workdays with both tangible and conceptual streamlining finesse will keep us caught-up right to the finish line. Caught up does not mean completed. It means we have control of the status and are clear on the next steps. Our communications are current. We are poised for tomorrow and pick up where we know we have left off. We are trackers and track ourselves as well.

Volunteers

The effective use of volunteers in our offices can help us to streamline our days. Truth be told - volunteers are to be revered. As William Shakespeare quoted, *"The meaning of life is to find your gift. The purpose of life is to give it away."* The giving of free time? That would be a yes. People who volunteer promote both goodness and progress and are true expressions of altruism. Hopefully in your organization, orientation and training covers your volunteer population. Regardless, administrative offices would benefit by holding a specific briefing for this group of amazing givers.

Prepare for investment if we want to retain our volunteer base. I know many people who don't draw on this population because the turnover is too frequent. Training time is spent, and the return is minimal. Like any investment, promoting growth and sustainability within our volunteer pool requires us to have a willing, clear, and favorable start. If the fit seems mutually agreeable, set a trial period of time. This way, there is a simple exit or enter strategy for both parties.

So, moving forward cohesively is decided. The adjective *cohesive* comes from the Latin word *cohaerere*, or *to cleave together*. Assistants establish these kinds of relationships all the time, volunteers included. Set a cool, calm, and collected pace and tour the physical space first. Keep tasks to a minimum and simplistic, i.e., phone system, office etiquette, and confidentiality expectations. Supply volunteers with key and foundational information like the vision/mission/values statement, internal communication and other directories, and board member names so that the volunteers can begin to learn who is who, what is what and when is time. Offer frequent and unwavering support. Convince volunteers that lists aside, most knowledge will come from the experience of being in the office over time. It would be impossible to teach all of the characteristic peculiarities and technicalities that occur in our offices because of the variety of circumstances that triggers our day's outcome. In hindsight, I have found that volunteers are more fulfilled by being part of the intelligent leadership environment than the actual tasks they perform. What makes volunteers happy will make us happy and motivation works nicely on a two-way street. Cater their responsibilities to what it is that they *want* to do. I know someone who has a pool of four volunteers per week; currently their terms of service at 3, 11, 13 and 18 years. They work in administration in northeast America, in a seasonal location where the population quadruples at tourist time. They are travelers and some are snowbirds who head south for the winter. They are knowledgeable, lovely, wise, funny, interesting, and willing. They represent the organization with the highest regard. This particular Assistant must prepare for their mass exodus in winter months since they have grown to handle much. Suddenly, filing, check requests, huddle notes, supplies, collating, phones and the like, must be absorbed by the Assistant or wait for spring. Beware of valuable volunteers.

"Volunteering is the ultimate exercise in democracy. You vote in elections once a year, but when you volunteer, you vote every day about the kind of community you want to live in."
-Author Unknown

Indeed, the utilization of volunteers aids in streamlining and has beautiful multi-faceted benefits for all involved.

Logistics and Streamlining Wrap-Up

Workspace rationale and streamlining improvement opportunities are abundant in growing businesses. If we take a bit of time to look around and think, we can see that they exist in short, mid, and long-term positions. So, let's have our overnight mail supplies on hand because when we have accomplished the near-impossible job of preparing documents to be sent next day/ first delivery, and we have 15 minutes before drop-off deadline, we need to have the flippin envelope and pre-paid form. Let's have a quick-reference orientation sheet for our volunteers. Let's utilize a desk file organizer in our boss's office that is set up with

Monday through Sunday folders. When boss sees "relevant note" on the calendar that says, "see Wednesday folder", all necessary information is already in that folder. Let's make the time to think about both tangible and conceptual streamlining processes and then upgrade them to more sensible standards.

Let's go back to 1868 for a moment and notice the *line drawn from point to point, so that its direction is everywhere that of the motion of the fluid.* Streamlining is all encompassing and marries nicely with our logical workspace environments. Work it. Worth it. Value it.

Proficiency and Preparedness.

Says it all. Best mouse EVER.

CHAPTER 6
Communication

I was so excited to write about communication until I considered it. The topic overwhelmed me. It felt too big, so ample time was spent in contemplation. My motivation to write about it returned when I concluded that communication in the simplest of terms is information exchange that determines outcomes and its importance to success is undeniable. Ah . . . if only communication didn't run the risk of complexity!

Communication is as vast and deep as the oceans of the Earth. The Pacific Ocean comes to mind. It is the largest of the world ocean basins, covering approximately 63 million square miles. All the world's continents could fit into the Pacific basin. The Mariana Trench located in the western Pacific Ocean is the deepest point in the world's oceans. The maximum known depth is 10,994 meters (36,070 feet) and is known as the *Challenger Deep*. That is as wide and deep as it gets – that we know of! In any event, it is as wide and deep as are the potentials for positive, negative, and everything in between communications. If sound communication skills were consistently taught in the home and throughout *all* children's education, and into adulthood, our world might look differently because our relationships would have more value. The good news: Communication skills can be improved with thought and practice at any point in our lives. Whew!

So, where will great communication get us? Answer: Everywhere we want to be. It can create movement, emotions, and a sense of comradery. This powerful word *camaraderie* made its first appearance in English in the mid-19th century. It comes from *camarade* in Middle French and was used to mean *roommate, companion,* or *a group sleeping in one room.* The *–ry* was not added in English until almost 40 years after *camaraderie.* Nowadays, it is more defined as *a spirit of friendly good fellowship.* To have this genial dynamic in the home, at work, and throughout our lives . . . well, I imagine the possibilities would be limitless.

We dialogue and monologue to accomplish results. We cheer, release, entertain, debate, educate, involve, cause or add to problems, and provide solutions. Communication is the only word I can think of that when we don't do it, we are still doing it. It far exceeds the act of speaking and not communicating can be both harshly and lovingly loud. Speech aside, our body language communicates volumes.

Drum roll please . . . because then comes the reactions to our verbal and non-verbal communications, which are driven by perceptions that have everything to do with the style of communication we own and one's view of our unique selves. Our expressions are meant as we know them and not always perceived in the way we intend. The word *intention* is rooted in Latin and in Old French is *entencion,* meaning *stretching, purpose.* Our delivery may not reflect our purpose, likely due to pressures we have. Added to our communication outcomes are the distinct personalities behind both the sender and the receiver. Communication is as powerful as it is sensitive and travels at varying speeds and all directions. It can level, destroy, and produce.

At times, Assistants respond to quick-firing calls that can jump from the benign to the extreme. Someone is calling to donate a half-million dollars and someone else is calling about an over 180-days past-due invoice. A board member is looking to speak with our boss and a vendor is trying to sell us a contract management system while the volunteer fire department is requesting physicals. Another person is confirming contact information for eighteen managers while at the same time we get a call regarding the rental of a property. I remember being on the phone addressing and tracking a complaint when another call came in requesting immediate assistance because a barge was sinking in the Atlantic Ocean and medical supplies were needed. The helicopter was already on route. I remember listening to someone's too-long winded account of an experience that they had when the alarm rang, and a Code Pink was called. Stimulation. Rapid thought and decisive action. Communication transmissions abound. Ahhhhhhh. It is much to manage. We Assistants are reference centers, we are bridge builders, we are visionary, we are responders, we are team members, and we are leaders.

Through some research and much reflection, three subsections emerged from the communication ocean:

- *We Receive and We Give*
- *Communication Specifics*
- *Presence and Wholeness*

Let's jump in.

We Receive and We Give

Regarding two- or multi-way communications, both articulation and definition run a fast mile. While shared pleasantries build productive and positive human connection outcomes, extra and irrelevant details can damper yield and tick us and people off. We usually know something of our audience when we prepare to communicate whether we are initiating the conversation or are on the receiving end of it. We can quickly tune-in. How we sound on the phone with a disgruntled client varies greatly from speaking with the deli person when placing an order because Ms. Anders is concerned about finances or a loved one and Big-Joe is super-excited to tell us about the new and ultimate sandwich platter. There is not one recipe to follow when we are giving or receiving meaningful communication but getting someone's full attention and trust is a must. Achieving this essential can be overlooked and communication will then be off to a compromised start. Accomplishing this essential gives a mission its best chance and can prove elemental in its execution. More on getting someone's attention in a bit.

When on the receiving end of communication, first and foremost, hard-core listening is paramount. Hear words. Hear tone. Zone in. We might think we do this but as distractions swarm our minds, we can become multi-directional. If we think we hear perhaps 77.5 percent, then I'd venture to say that we might just get 77.5 percent

66

to the goal and that is a C+. We know what it feels like when we are the initiators of communication and we can sense that we are only partially being heard. It's frustrating. What happens when we are at 100 percent is buy-in because after we really listen, our response is clear and connecting. The person becomes disarmed and immediately knows that they have our undivided attention and that we are there to help. We cannot fake this 100% . . . does not work. I can't emphasize enough how we can go from first to fourth gear in an incredibly short amount of time by choosing to give the 100 percent when it comes to the listening aspect of communication. A form of trust and fluidity is quickly established. Quite frankly, we can end up telling someone something that they don't even want to hear but one, they have been educated, and two, they have retained their integrity. This establishes a mutuality. It is fair and is super-sized productive. More on integrity later in this chapter under *Presence and Wholeness.*

While responding to received information is one thing, our outgoing communications are what cues up and pushes our initiatives backward or forward.

Getting someone's attention and trust at the onset of communication cuts to the chase. How we sound, our posture, and our vibrations (the energy we throw off) gives others a preview of what's to come. Others don't just hear it or see it. They feel it. There is an innate response from the receiver that occurs instantly.

Sound. Posture. Vibrations.

Sound. We, like techies, aim to get the best sound possible for listening pleasure and potency.

Take the sound bar, which has many evolving features, like the Dynamic Range Control (DRC). It provides dynamic range compression for Dolby Digital content to make the sound clearer when the volume is at a low level. Hmmmm, this seems like it can be an effective way to communicate. Another feature of the sound bar is the Adaptive Sound Control (ASC), allowing devices to automatically change sound settings to suit a range of media types in order to get the most out of a wide variety of content. Awesome if we can accomplish this adaption feature in our communications. How we sound sets a path for what is to come.

Posture. Just the other day I passed an office where an employee in a new position was covering phones in their new department. I said, "Welcome and congratulations on your new job! New position – wow, seems like there is a lot of opportunity for you!" And this is what I saw. The employee slouched way back in the desk chair, big smile on her face, weight leaning on her elbow and a sort of *yup I'm all that and more* look on her face. Ugh. Not good. Hopefully someone will take advantage of a teaching opportunity and help this kid out. I missed my opportunity but will stay alert when another one presents itself. I imagine this bright kid has a lot to offer.

Conversely, there is a concierge employee who often deals with a high volume of interactions that occur simultaneously in the main lobby. He presents himself as present, astute, focused (eye-contact), and is clearly both knowledgeable and pleasant. He works his movement area well and all on the receiving end are dealt with as individuals and are directed accordingly and assuredly. Assistants are frontline too, which is where confidences begin, and directional movement occurs.

Occasionally, let's self-check our posture throughout the course of our days. We want to present ourselves as ready. The correct manner of sitting/standing/walking keeps our body systems aligned. Our main (and plentiful!) body systems include circulatory, digestive, endocrine, integumentary, lymphatic, muscular, nervous,

68

renal, reproductive, respiratory, and skeletal. Let's take care of all of them and keep our channels clear. It is the well-oiled system that can outperform.

Vibrations. For now, I'll just leave it at this: We all know that how we feel sends wavelengths outward. See Chapter 8, *And Who Am I?*, for more detailed information on the relationships between the mind, drive, body, and heart. This package throws off everything from gloom to sparkle.

"Invisible airwaves
Crackle with life
Bright antennae bristle
With the energy
Emotional feedback
On a timeless wavelength
Bearing a gift beyond price
Almost free"
Spirit of Radio
– RUSH

Communication Specifics

Following are some basic communication tools and techniques to keep in our pockets. This subsection covers common misused phrases, inclusivity and charge, internal communication directories, openers/closers/contents, and, interest and momentum . . . all as they relate to the effectiveness of our communications.

Common Misused Phrases. First let's cover some common phrases and words that are often used incorrectly. Here are but a smidgen of some that I come across:

1. For all *intensive purposes* should be for *all intents and purposes.*

2. *In regards to* should be *in regard to*: When introducing a topic, this phrase is singular.

3. *Irregardless* should be *regardless*, meaning without regard. *Irregardless* is not a word. Adding the *'ir'* prefix creates a double negative and would mean *without without regard*.

4. Use the word *who* if we can replace it with *he* or *she* and use the word *whom* if we can replace it with *him* or *her*.

5. When trying to convey that we have made a reversal on an issue, we are *doing a 180 degree turn* (not a *360*). A *360* would illustrate that where we got to, was where we started, i.e., doing a donut while driving. Gets you nowhere.

6. If something is irrelevant it is *moot point* (not *mute point*). *Mute* is a button on our remote control!

7. Let's be sure to *flesh it out*, and not *flush it out*. *Flesh it out* adds to the understanding or development of a concept while *flush it out* removes rather than adds. We all know what image to use to remember that one!

8. When talking about results, use *effect* (typically a noun), and use *affect* (typically a verb), when there is a notion of influence.

9. *Disinterested* means unbiased. It does not mean *uninterested*.

10. *Fortuitous* is happening by chance, which could be good or bad, while *fortunate* is happening by luck, which is always good.

Inclusivity and Charge. Another specific tool to incorporate into our performance is the commitment to inclusivity and charge. When taking or giving written or verbal messages, give them some charge by not only including the obvious (name, contact, date, time), but also note the basic point, question and/or next step. Hang up with or write down the understood upcoming action, especially when it comes to expected time frames. This important practice of accomplishing the task at hand while creating clear next steps (also referenced in Chapter 2, *The Art and Psychology of Scheduling Meetings* and Chapter 5, *Logistics and Streamlining*), is paramount to our ability to accelerate and accomplish. In our communications, ask all pertinent questions and give all information the first time out. Sounds easier than it sometimes is simply because our minds track much. How many times do we finally get a few minutes with our boss to cover items and the moment we get back to our desk in relief mode, we realize there is that one topic we did not address. Often the curtain closes before we can re-enter stage left. Another file to sit in the first violin position on our desk, aside from our active meeting coordination file, is the one we grab when we have the opportunity (scheduled or not) to meet and review all kinds of information with our boss. Keeping a page paper-clipped to the front of the file where we can jot down notes to communicate is wise, especially as items and thoughts strike us when we are in the middle of something else. Having pen and post-its on this accessible file will equip us to maximize this boss-meeting opportunity. Fully loaded is to efficiency as partiality is to deficiency.

Email communications work best when they are clear, charged, and all-inclusive. When we are at the glorious point of confirming a meeting via email, note the previously held dates so the receiver can immediately omit them from their calendars. We have all been in the position where we happen upon numerous held timeframes only to finally figure out that a particular meeting had already been confirmed. Also, add the phone, videoconference, in-person, and dial-in information directly in the body of the email or Invite. Let's keep our go-to stamps well inked: DRAFT; COPY; MAILED; CONFIDENTIAL; E-MAILED; and, RECEIVED. This is all a part of good communication. Forethought and practice will improve our ability to grow and round-out our communication performance.

Regarding the charge part of inclusivity, I loved receiving this communication from a friend/co-worker who sent a message to all staff: "Just a reminder, if you are interested in attending the Annual Party you **must** buy your tickets by December 5th. This year **no** tickets will be sold **after December 5th**." Cracked me up. Point made.

Internal Communication Directories. The Internal Communication Directory is a specific tool that is not to be undervalued. This listing is sterling silver to Assistants, although it will quickly lose its brilliant luster if not consistently updated. Hopefully in your organization the responsible party for this directory realizes the importance of sensible, comprehensive, and accurate information. If not, consider investing in yourself becoming this responsible party. We become a wealth of information when we can count on our internal directory.

Openers. Closers. Contents. Our communications are packaged up with these three specific components. This package opens with a salutation that sets a tone. Hi Friend . . . [Name] . . . Hello! . . . [Nothing] . . . Good Afternoon, Dear Esteemed Committee, etc. The *very first* response to our communication is determined by our opener. Openers are not necessary, but they do add to the quality of forming a tone and a hopeful united whole.

Closers wrap up the package. In email, there is the forever go-to, Sincerely. Then there's the: Warm Regards, Thank You or Thank You Kindly, With Appreciation, As Always, and Wishing You Best Regards,. Oh yes, let's not forget, Best,. I recently received Best with 5 exclamation points!!!!! Sometimes we opt to close with nothing while other times we just use our names. We choose to sign-off in various ways depending on our mood, the person/people, and the point. There was a closing of a Masters of Health Administration Program. The notice was undeniably heart-felt, and it concluded with, Warmly and with gratitude,. It was appropriate and touching. At times we can be tempted to close with something more like: Farewell, You've Got to be Kidding Me, Stop, Needing a Break, or

Over a Whiskey,. These non-options can happily flow through our minds. Captain Obvious says it is good to find a closer that is both appropriate and truthful.

Although communications have tone-setting openers and closers, it is everything in the middle that importantly determines effectiveness. Content. Sometimes we decide to put out the mass scheduling request only after availability is confirmed for particular attendees. For instance, I received an email with this content: "Based on the calendars of x/y/z, the best date options for the Integration Meeting are 1/2/3 . . . at [location]. Please advise of your respective executive's availability." This Assistant already has a jump on the game. Then he rounds-out and lists all the Assistants names next to the executive's names and thanks us all. The Assistant continues to keep us posted. This middle work is the energy of consensus. We all get it – we are all with you comrade. (Much more on consensus later in this chapter.)

Interest and Momentum. There is another specific technique to use that is less tangible and more action oriented. It is the routine practice of keeping interest and momentum alive and well. *"Hi so and so . . . just to let you know I should hear from so and so by mid-day tomorrow and should be able to confirm the Webinar. Stay tuned."* People in the know tend to be content and retain motivation. I'd venture to say that these status reports in turn nurture quick responses. Optimized Assistants keep the energy going. Is it always necessary to take the time under some circumstances to give this kind of status report? No. Is it a worthwhile investment? Indeed, it is.

Speaking of keeping communication alive, Administrative offices are similar to airport traffic control towers. It is a main hub where direction, instruction, and information are disseminated. It can be frustrating when we hear people claim that they were not aware about something whether it be a new service, an event, an open enrollment date, or a new process that has been implemented.

It is especially frustrating when we know the information has already been relayed through various channels like emails, bulletin boards, meetings, newsletters, and town hall meetings. To get communications out to our organizations is easy compared to having them be read, heard, and absorbed. It requires a culture change if the staff at large is feeling that they lack knowledge. Let's say that is the case. What is missing? Excitement. Gratification. Eagerness. A shared and understood goal. Sporting events are testimony to a team's determination. Each member brings their "A" game and fully supports each other. The result is a revved engine. Players want to be part of the effort. It is much simpler to establish this dynamic in sporting events than in our work organizations, but it is no less necessary for goal attainment. Where do Assistants fall in this effort? We need to set by example. We need to be consistent. At times, we need to send out reminder notifications if need be. Example: An Information Technology department is frustrated because staff kept coming to them for their computer needs and they did not follow the already circulated process for completing tickets that had been in place for a year. Some items, like this one, need quarterly reminders from us until a new norm takes hold. Assistants need to bring their "A" game to communication actions so that all share in motivation and excitement. People do want to be part of winning teams. Assistants are critical to this momentum. Our reactions and responses affect others. The health of our organization depends on leaders who set by example.

"Throw your soul through every open door . . ."
-Adele

Presence and Wholeness

Our communications have an impact on the progress our organizations are hungry for. We need to act or respond amid varying situations that always require us to be adaptable.

Optimized Assistants are very present and really have no choice but to stay in the here and now. Yes, other levels operate for planning purposes, but we admirably exist in a state of unwavering availability. This can be tough because we must live in perpetual communication-land. There is no getting away from it. There are times when we have said to ourselves, "What?? . . . Am I the full-time point person in a library's reference section??" Well, despite the burden this can present at times, I hope we all feel that way because it means we are doing our job well by rendering and representing. Anyone who has a question, any question, bring it on. We know the answer, or we know where to find it. We know we can rely on ourselves and we know we spend our days in educating and improving the mission of our organization by serving in the capacity of *Information Center*.

Two situations and one conviction follow that address presence and wholeness: communication in difficult situations, communication in group settings, and . . . da-da-dada! . . . the power of consensus as it relates to positive communication outcomes. After all, notable progress is not realized if communication wholeness is not achieved.

Communication in Difficult Situations. We are involved in a project with a pressured deadline. We answer the phone because we must, and a worker asks us to verify a long list of contacts. A highly agitated person walks into our office making demands. A vendor walks into our office unannounced. A person who recently lost a loved one shows up to understand health benefit responsibilities. A former employee appears at the door to speak with the administrator. Three sets of people simultaneously arrive at our office each wanting our attention. These are situations that we can find ourselves in.

I have heard from many of us that navigating through these unpleasant milieus rank high regarding our job dissatisfaction.

Unequivocally understandable. When confronted with these types of circumstances our innate reaction can look like any number of caution and hazard signs. Added is our emotional reaction that says to us ugh . . . grrrrr.

Enter once again the powerful mind that can turn these varying circumstances into positive human connections. We can choose to see the opportunity for solution instead of the problem. Easy to say but it really does take some practice to train our minds to have an improved initial reaction become our pattern when addressing difficult situations.

So how do we accomplish opportunistic view attainment? Here is my recipe. When we approach and address all situations with the intention only to meet on level ground, then the fearful part of these interactions cease to exist. From level ground we can begin healthy dialogue. Important - the other person(s) do not need to be on level ground and chances are they are not, otherwise it would not be counted as a difficult situation. On level ground, we disarm and are patient and present. The freezer begins to defrost. If the circumstance is not contentious but has degrees of anxiety associated with it, then chances are high that the anxiety will melt away because all that is really happening is much simpler than we make it out to be. Look at it this way. Two people are meeting, and dialogue ensues. If focus stays on the point and not the emotion, then solution is in reach. We must be steadfast in our position to stay on level ground. This is where forward movement can occur. Yes, it ties directly to respect. People are just doing their jobs or looking for an answer. They deserve our full attention. Communication is not difficult when it is fair. Assistants, we are in a role where we can conduct our orchestra. What music score do we choose to present? I know we prefer triumph over tragedy and the thrill of victory over the agony of defeat. And to be less dramatic, maybe what is preferred by all is to communicate absent of judgement.

Communication in Group Settings. Following are three group setting communication dynamics: the good, the bad, and the beautiful.

The Good. In 1978 there was a high-school student named Devon, who was in his theater class. The class of twelve were given instructions for an exercise in communication and control. All students were asked to sit on the floor in a circle. The professor set a timer for three minutes and the students were asked to communicate with each other with the goal to be the person in control of the conversation at the close of the three minutes. Timer set and "Go" was called. Here is what happened. Nancy went on a tirade, Chuck tried to quiet her so he could make his point, Alfonso attempted to reason, and all else ventured to chime in and command. It was loud and chaotic. Devon was the only one who sat quietly and deliberately watched each participant, one at a time. He held his gaze, one by one. He began to be noticed. Five seconds before the timer binged, he calmly raised both his posture and a hand. All froze and directed their attention to him. He quietly said, "Hi". He had the full attention of the group and the situation was in the palm of his hand.

The Bad. I experienced an ultra-fail due to my success in sinking my own battleship through poor communication. I was scheduled for my performance appraisal. The form was already completed by my boss and process dictated a sit-down review of scores, including a written evaluation paragraph. This was followed by optional discussion and sealed by signatures and date at conclusion. This anecdote can also apply under Chapter 7, *The Value of the Hard Lessons Learned*, but for now, let's just say that my glowing evaluation was flattened and flipped like a burnt pancake. Why? Well, during the optional discussion, I shared excessively tense and over-hyped communication about some of my opinions. I was professionally immature and misdirected. My intention was to be productive and my delivery was not. I was responsible for a dialogue that spiraled downward. It was the oddest of moments to sign my stellar evaluation with tears streaming and nerves short-circuiting. Yes, we learn in hard ways at times and communication can most certainly alter outcomes.

Here is another Bad. At an elementary school in a small, robust town in north central New Hampshire, there was a scheduling meeting that was attended by teachers and special educators with the goal to create the ideal day's schedule for the kids by grade level, Pre-K through Sixth. "You are the kings and queens of schedules!" teachers were told by administration. Meeting began. A teacher made a salient and justified point about where music and art should occur in the schedule. Shot down by the special educators. Another teacher articulated a benefit of math early on, pre-recess. Shot down again. And so, it went. The special educators who spent an important yet a fraction of the days' time with the children were intent on a microcosm view of just their purpose. No big picture, no consideration, no mediator. The meeting ended with no conclusion except a waste of everyone's time.

"Communication breakdown
It's always the same
I'm having a nervous breakdown
Drive me insane!"
Led Zeppelin (released in 1969)

Communication has no bridge when attention and consideration are absent, even despite the presence of an assumed shared goal. Sides cannot cross over and be joined. Well, keep the faith. After all, chocolate and peanut butter did meet as very different individuals, were discovered to be complimentary in their relationship, and work VERY well together. We don't all need to be alike to make it happen. Ask a raisin, ice cream or a strawberry. Listen, consider, and

78

be cooperative. Cooperative. Latin in origin, *cooperari, working together*. For those whose intent is single-minded, consider yourself as part of the problem.

The Beautiful. My Dad witnessed many meetings and speeches at the New York City restaurant *21 Club* where he worked as a waiter for thirty-five years. His brood of five children often and excitedly asked him whom he had seen at the restaurant who was famous. Although he was incredibly impressed by Martina Navratilova's forearm girth, he cared much less about who was who. Instead, his steel blue eyes would widen, and his face would come alive as he told us about some relative unknown who when speaking had the undivided attention of both audience and restaurant staff alike. He kept our attention because we were caught up in his excitement about the delivery and manner of the speaker. The degree of success of a good communicator, whether it be from the famous, not so famous, or someone like my Dad, can easily be measured by the sensations that receivers feel from the cores of their mind and heart. Attention salutes.

The Power of Consensus. Mid-century Latin meaning *agreement*. It seems the greatest progression occurs when consensus is achieved. A strengthening dynamic results when the three crucial elements to the functioning of consensus are present: (1) common acceptance of laws, rules, and norms, (2) attachment to the institutions, which promote and apply the laws and rules, and (3) a widespread sense of identity or unity, which discloses to individuals who experience it. Those features are identical and therefore equal. I've come to find out that there is a ginormous amount of materials, studies, and opinions out there regarding consensus. It struck me that in simple terms consensus equals progress and peace.

The world population was estimated to have reached 7.7 billion as of October 2019. The United Nations estimates it will further increase to 9.4 billion by the year 2100. Just one billion equals one thousand million, or 1,000,000,000. Quite unbelievable to know that clones are not a part of these totals. Just imagine what would come if agreement was reached on even one item for 7.7 billion people. Reality is such that we experience face-to-face consensus challenges, let alone those within family units, communities, states, countries, and continents. We are not meant to agree on everything, nor would we want to. Life would be horribly boring and dull. Yet we could use more progress and peace . . . agree? Ok. Likely, our world population has a high consensus on that.

The value of consensus and the opportunity for sound communication are undervalued as breakthrough ingredients for all kinds of advancement. Question - Who goes to work to have a bad day? There you go. Consensus.

Communication Wrap-Up

If our work communications are an aggregate of both clear and necessary information and honest drive, then coping with what is at hand and what is to come becomes achievable, gratifying, and even exciting. Thought and practice investments. Articulation and definition advantages. Hard-core listening requirements. Guides and channels tools. Our condition and connection relationships. Inclusivity and charge results. Sound/Posture/Vibrations effects. Clear, complete, and necessary information benefits. Momentum, consensus, attention, and trust essentials. Integrity, respect, and honesty jackpots. Yes . . . it is all determined by the overall state of our presence.

The most admirable communicators and the ones most heard are not the loudest nor the most intense and certainly not anyone with anger. So, what is involved in mastering this communication/being heard skill? It can be realized through: Practice; Desire; Preparation; Patience; Pacing; Belief; and, Trust. Great speakers have a steadfast synergy with their audience, and they listen back and feel the honesty in both sound and silence.

Assistants who are optimized invest in nurturing their many relationships through the quality or state of being focused, genuine, and honest in their communications. Here is why the investment works. First, it feels good. Secondly, when we need something badly and quickly, we want to be met with a "sure – no problem – need anything else?" response. We get what we give. Value of all kinds flourishes.

"It's not whatcha got, it's what you give
It ain't the life you choose, it's the life you live
It's only what you give, only what you give, only what you give
It's not whatcha got, but the life you live.
-Tesla

Investing thought and practice in communication skills can bring us to the top of mountains with great results. Thankfully, I have several accomplishments that have been realized through the basic ability to share effectively. The point I want to make though, is that how we communicate is reflective of what our condition is at any given point in time, leaving the field wide open to strike out or score. So, although it's great to drill down on our communication techniques, let's remember that effectiveness is really born from the healthy qualities of being focused, honest, prepared, calm, and genuine. When communication's condition is unified and unimpaired in its construction, there is integrity for the communicator. *Integrity* from French *integrite* or Latin *integritas* means intact and is defined as the quality of being honest and having strong moral principles. Moral uprightness. Wow. This word is not to be taken lightly. When the whole is larger than the sum of the parts, creativity and progress occur. When the whole is smaller than the sum of the parts, we have breakdown. Yes, communication can level, destroy, and produce. Honoring integrity through our communication not only adds value to us in the workplace, it adds value to peace among us.

More on integrity. It is said that my grandfather could wear an oversized rummage sale coat and present himself to the Queen on foundationally equal grounds. Although there are understandable and necessary parameters to follow regarding position rank, all sound and optimized human connections respectfully meet in balance.

"Out beyond ideas of wrongdoing and rightdoing
there is a field. I'll meet you there."
-Rumi

We all know how technology advances have both constrained and liberated us. Our life balance can be jeopardized by rapid pace and yet the world has been opened to us. Like the vast and deep oceans of the Earth, communication is a force that can rock our worlds. Let's give it its rightful power.

CHAPTER 7
The Value of Hard Lessons Learned

What is failure all depends on our *choice* regarding point of view. We all know that great leaders have made their fair share of major mistakes. Look them up: Abraham Lincoln, Nelson Mandela, Steve Jobs, Alexander the Great . . . on and on. Makes for some interesting reading and can remind us that we are not alone. Even huge mistakes are surmountable. Mistakes can bite hard at the time of experiencing consequences. They can negatively affect our sense of self-worth or they can build character and gift enhancement when addressed. Our choice.

The word *address* in Latin is *ad-directus* and in Old French and Middle English means *set upright*. The sooner we address the better. Time lapses, excuses, and blamers open up a world of complication. I once had a boss who I'll name *Mr. Itold Yuso*. Big mistake for one, especially for a leader, to consistently stand (wherever!) with hands in pockets, head down, nodding parallel to the floor while announcing that the world would be a better place if people just listened to him. Respect barometer major drop. This is just one kind of mistake. It's a leadership-approach mistake and his time served was short-lived. For that and other reasons, the departure was quick and not by choice.

There are the more tangible mistakes like jumping hierarchy. It can be difficult, albeit wise, to verbalize our personal and significant issues through good communication with our direct reports, even if it is uncomfortable for us to do so. If it is time to include next levels of leadership, then let's consider being transparent about our predicaments. The fear related to facing this kind of exposure sure beats the harshly strained scenario of secretly going behind backs. Exceptions to jumping hierarchy? Sure. Think carefully and proceed cautiously.

Accept. Admit. Address. (aka A.A.A.) It is the confident Assistant that accepts, admits and addresses mistakes head-on. Think about it. How can solutions be found if confronting and coming to terms with mistakes do not occur? Call it anything we want ... making an error, blunder, howler, or misjudgment. Making mistakes does not mean that we are perceived as inadequate or unsuitable. On the contrary, admittance plays toward adequacy and suitability. There is *always* a solution. Even when just months ago, while fighting panic, I had to abandon my car in a full force blizzard with whiteout conditions. It was a big misjudgment on my part to drive in this monster of a storm. We should never put ourselves in dire straits. No matter the situation, we should place our mind management focused on answers, especially in extreme conditions. What is interesting and fortunate for us is how we can cause problems and yet choose to use them as opportunities for improvement. It was time anyway to put to rest my 2002 Ford Focus that I had been driving for eight years. Deliberate calculation with a bit of faith left me with new wheels that I never cease to appreciate. Moreover, I will never be found driving (in any car!) in a blizzard again. Harsh lesson learned. When we put ourselves in self-imposed predicaments in our jobs, we will have to work too hard and for too long to get it back to what we want it to be. Avoid mistakes where possible and when we do falter - accept, admit, and address to move forward.

More on A.A.A. Take this locksmith person. He works in a school system and like many of us, he learned much on the job. He had two formal hours of training and support, but education and progress would need to be self-driven. He was all heart and focus when it came to the importance of safety and security for all. What existed was an antiquated database for locks with nineteen swipe cards that were manually assigned to specific access rights for approximately two hundred people. One lock needed to be deleted from the software program since it was no longer in use. *Delete Lock* was the intended next move and *Delete Account* was inadvertently clicked. Realizing the error of wiping out the entire institution's security access system, the locksmith's mind jumped to recovery mode. Recycle bin. No go - since it was a high security program that was an exception to the Windows general path to move actions to recycle. Ok. Next recovery option. Contact the software technician. After explaining what had happened, there was a deafening silence, and the technician's exact words were, "Oh. Sorry man, there's no way to recover the information. Although the upgraded software version enables a recovery, this one does not." Uh oh. Remaining recovery option. The system back-up. Come to find out, the last back-up occurred two years prior. Enter - serious moment of truth. There is that moment where fear and nerves thrive in the pit of the stomach. So, what did the locksmith do? He walked into the director's office, shut the door behind him, took off his ID badge and placed it on the director's desk, therefore surrendering his role. Told him everything that happened. He took full accountability. Painful silence. Then, the director asked one thing, "What do you need to fix it?" The locksmith answered, "Three weeks, a software program that I've researched, an office, and title change." He added that last request with a rather uncomfortable chuckle. Here is how it played out.

The locksmith got the three weeks, an office, the title change, and the building security access system was revamped and designed as a Level 4 master keying system. Consider the outcome if the locksmith did not walk into the director's office that day, place his badge on his desk, and then choose the route of honest and full disclosure. Hard lessons learned can only begin when we first choose to accept, admit, and then address our mistakes.

Much more difficult are those mistakes we make where our ego is involved. There are people who are book-smart abundant while they lack practical knowledge and basic kindness. There is a human connection disconnect. The ego can become the mistake, like the time mine was rooted in assumed self-importance. Ugh. Deep breath. Well, I can't tell you much because as hard as I've tried, I can't remember the specifics. It must be a survival instinct to forget negatives. It was approximately eight years ago. What is important though, is what I do remember of it. While I was riding high on my horse, I was overheard by my boss when speaking to one of his colleagues. I remember that I was not being secretive nor scheming. I was, though, full of some serious addi-paddi (that's slang for attitude). Not appropriate. My mistake was a blessing in disguise, one that when being called out on it, felt far from anything resembling a blessing. To me, it felt like I took an upper cut to the jaw and it resulted in a personal, emotional knockdown. I did get up from the ground and am better for it. I (after some time) thanked my boss for setting me straight on that situation because it served as a hard, yet valuable, lesson learned. The origin of the idiom *blessing in disguise* is believed to be mid-1700s. Scholars have yet to pin down the first usage of the term. Oscar Wilde's *The Importance of Being Ernest* includes this: "And now, Dear Mr. Worthing, I will not intrude any longer into a house of sorrow. I would merely beg you not to be too much bowed down by grief. What seem to us bitter trials are often blessings in disguise." Are mistakes and difficult situations blessings in disguise? Yes, if we let them be that.

"Come December, the sun barely makes an appearance. The cold, dark winters can be challenging, but adapting to the changing season is a way to stay mindful."
-Swedish

Forbes (2015) lists nine of the worst mistakes we can ever make at work as: telling lies, gossiping, announcing that we hate our job, having an emotional hijacking (throwing things, screaming), taking credit for someone else's work, bragging, backstabbing, eating smelly food, and burning bridges. I would add another one to that list: treating difficult situations with contentious vigor instead of using great care. As obvious as these *do-not-do's* are, we can become unfortunate subjects to their threats. What to do about it? Let's consider the *Adaption Theory*.

Adaption Theory. If there is ever a corner we need to turn, it is the one when we falter. It's relatively easy to know we need to adapt after conflict but not always so easy to do it. Post falter, we experience the stop-points: anger, disappointment, and regret, which initially come into play. Like *Maslow's Hierarchy of Needs* theory (1943), it seems these emotions must take hold before we can step out and up. This reaction phase can be brief or lengthy and can include anything under the sky including tears, fears, emptiness, depression, and too much ice cream with too many toppings.

Adaption Theory (aka Survival Theory) is an organism's ability to adapt to changes in its environment and adjust accordingly over time. There are three habitat changes that can occur: habitat, genetic, or extinction. When we falter, we do not want to *habitat change* because then we would just find another environment similar to the one we are in. *Genetic change* would be great but unfortunately, we are not like the turtles in the Galapagos Islands who morphed to longer legs and necks to reach a new food source.

Lastly, when a species is unable to move or change, it will become *extinct*. We certainly don't want that!

Consider that we can apply the adaption theory to help survive our self-imposed difficult situations. Adaptions can occur internally, like vertebrates who have adapted to be able to regulate their body temperatures. Although this adaption theory is based on physical changes, the idea of internal adaption can be applied to times that we mentally and emotionally need to turn that corner and convert a sour into a sweet. It starts in our brains and it can inhabit our hearts. What is failure all depends on our *choice* regarding point of view. The fact that we can choose our perspective, can use time in our favor, and can surrender in order to evolve from our mistakes, is something to treasure. It is where hard lessons become learned.

The Value of Hard Lessons Learned Wrap-up

Let's *set upright*, withstand any regret, and forge ahead with head held high and with a humbled gratitude for self-forgiveness, acceptance, conduct, and the faith that we can choose to move to fruitful outcomes and personal growth. It really is ok. Turning corners that trend toward improvement is obtainable through hard lesson learned. Operative word . . . learn. Grasp them. Don't fear them. Move on.

CHAPTER 8
And Who Am I?

Thankfully, this question can be addressed in the presence of our privacy, where we can be attentive, safe, and honest. While objectivity can play well when looking at our situations and relationships with others, objectivity can also support our self-growth and levels of fulfillment. I really don't know how I am perceived but I do know that who I am is dependent on how well I take care of my mind, drive, body, and heart. My end result at any given point in time is determined by the presence and conditions of these factors. The mind can drive, the body needs to keep up with both cognitive management and motivation, and the heart can lead.

The Mind

In the introduction, essential mind management is referenced. The word *essential* is Latin in origin, *essentialis*, and in Middle English means *in the highest degree*. Mind management plus highest degree equals openness, where we can find ourselves capable of what we may not have once thought possible. The power of being mindful can bring us to mountain peaks with unbelievable views. It develops confidence and offers paths, needed releases, and peace.

In 1941 there was a young boy who by no choice of his own assisted the Priest as an altar boy in his hometown church in Pernitz, Austria. He was a courageous one, riding life precisely on the edge of both lovability and trouble. He held the leadership role in the clan of little boys who lived adventurously in a mountain town located thirty-five miles southwest of Vienna. Post church, the boys had a routine that began with a stop at the corner store to buy ice cream cones and ended goodness knows where. One day, little 9-year old Conrad had a dilemma. It was a Sunday and he had no coins for his ice cream cone since his family lived by little means. While cleaning up communion, he found himself alone in the church kitchen lock-gazed on the offering collection from the service. Feeling the pressure of his reputation at stake with the boys, he uneasily took two coins, just enough to cover his ice cream cone and preserve his dignity. Enter another gaze, fierce in truth, and that which came from the Priest catching him red-handed in the act. Little Conrad quickly dropped the coins back in the offering plate and turned, head-down, to face his demise. After a frozen silence, the Priest, in a low and surprisingly neutral tone said, *"Warum nimmst du Geld von der Kirche?"* The Priest asked him why he took money from the Church. *"Eine Eistute kaufen"*, the boy admitted the reason. Another, even longer, frozen silence. The Priest's next and only move was to reach into his pocket and hand the boy two of his own coins. Little Conrad, as hard as he tried, could not bring himself to buy the ice cream cone. The following Sunday, the Priest's coins found their way back to the offering plate.

Clearly, some self-driven and decisive mind management occurred for the Priest. An abundance of mind management had to occur in little Conrad's brain. So, where did this experience leave the boy? Scared at the moment, yet ultimately, it left him on a mountain peak with a view that developed his consciousness and character. It offered him a path, a release, and eventual peace.

The Drive

Why drive? Maybe because life as we know it is short and we would like to play a part in its meaning, its beauty, its sustainability, and its progress. We drive because at times we believe it necessary, while other times we need to push to have our goals realized. What drives us is personal, sacred, and ours to determine and manage. Common denominator and truth be told, for all of us, "this ain't no dress rehearsal", as a good friend consistently reminds me. Our time here on planet Earth is but a blip. This is a good reason to drive.

Drive, born from necessity, is often realized without a lot of thought. When someone is in trouble, the instinct to kick in and help is immediate. When there is an organization hit with a power outage, a fire, a shooting, a flood or some such matter, people band together quickly. Most admirably, people rise immediately in the face of these kinds of events. Power is met with people-power on survival consensus. Admirable things occur. The drive is a given. It is already there.

It is a different story when drive is born from our choice in the matter. It can cause pause to stare indecisively and in perplexity at the too-many-choices cereal box isle in a grocery store, let alone deal with all of life's options that are there for us to decide. The mere magnitude of directions to take, let alone the drive to accomplish steps toward our goals and realize our visions, can be inordinate. It's no wonder it can be so easy to procrastinate, be stuck in the rut, ignore, and even give up. Who are we when we see and want, and yet stand there paralyzed at our self-built walls? Who are we when we balance, manage, try, and trust as we remove the bricks one by one? Who are we when we let fright rule and who are we when we opt to consider and act on faith?

Managing our drive comes with discipline and I was curious to read up on studies that address one's ability to exercise disciplines, for instance, the delay of gratification.

Take the Stanford marshmallow experiment. It was a series of studies on delayed gratification in the late 1960s and early 1970s led by psychologist Walter Mischel, then a professor at Stanford University. In these studies, children were offered choices between one small reward provided immediately and two small rewards if they waited for a short period, approximately 15 minutes, during which the tester left the room and then returned. (The reward was sometimes a marshmallow, but often a cookie or a pretzel.) In follow-up studies, which spanned more than 40 years, the researchers found that children who were able to wait longer for the double-goodie reward tended to have better life outcomes, as measured by SAT scores, lower levels of substance abuse, better responses to stress, educational attainment, body mass index, and other life measures. Some describe this outcome of success as choosing the pain of discipline over the ease of distraction. Of course, success and contentment are not that simple but nevertheless, the ability to choose mind discipline over immediate gratification seems to correlate with overall personal and professional achievement. The ability to discipline can in part affect our ability to motivate.

Also studied is the question on whether the ability to discipline is a predetermined and more natural ability or if it is more based on other factors of environment and upbringing. Researchers at the University of Rochester replicated the marshmallow experiment and added a new factor. The children were split into two groups. The first group was exposed to a series of unreliable experiences. For example, the researcher gave the child a box of crayons and promised to bring a bigger box, but never did. The second group was exposed to reliable experiences, where they were told they would receive another box of crayons and did. Just a few minutes of reliable (positive) or unreliable (negative) experiences were enough to push the actions of each child in one direction or another. Trust issues affected outcome. Granted, life is seriously more complex than this small insight but the good take-away from

92

this experiment is that the choice and ability to self-discipline will work for us as we aim to keep our motivation levels intact.

There is much literature to read regarding discipline improvement and it is worth the investment to educate ourselves on the good tools out there to raise this essential arm of success. Analogies compare things, typically for the purpose of explanation or clarification, so I say that discipline and confidence are to motivation as dedication and hope are to far-sighted faith.

Do we work with people who are driven mostly or only by personal gain? If not currently (whew), likely we have. Both the selfless individual who exercises discipline and the one who is narcissistic are driven. My experiences with self-centered people and especially those that drive from the notion of entitlement leave me starkly aware of their insecurities, lack of fulfillment, intense unease, clear instability, and great discontent. Let's not concern ourselves with them because they are very busy making their beds. Hopefully something eye-opening and mind-altering comes their way to negate the reasons for their kind of motivation. Consider that there are not either bad or good people, but those who are unwilling or those who are willing.

"Calmness, gentleness, silence, self-restraint, and purity: these are
the disciplines of the mind."
-Holy Bhagwad Geeta

The Body

Physical health. All right. I won't bore us with what we already know. Here is what I'm saying on the subject. Aside from the many benefits we know of exercise, (ooops starting to get boring!), so many of us release ourselves from this requirement of working toward and attaining our personal optimized condition. Our reasons for this are rightfully private, real, and certainly validated

93

but not ultimately justified. It is we who choose to thrive or to suffer the consequences. So here it is. It is discipline, patience, and belief. That is what exercise is. Period. We can *choose* to get there and yes, despite pushbacks born from fears of failure, it CAN BE that simple. Don't bite my head off with my choice to use the word *simple*. The word to focus on is *choose*. Choice is in our control and making a choice cannot be disingenuous. It is a humbling experience to have self-belief. At times, we must surrender our anxieties to move forward. Discipline, patience, and belief. Consider ten blank pages following this opinion because it can take a while to absorb simplicity.

My grandfather was a Presbyterian minister in Brooklyn, New York, who in large part, preached through parables. His sermons were both palpable and effective because taking or leaving a point from a story was for each to decide for themselves. No pressure. Nice way to grow. So, I can only tell you my story on what exercise does for me and feel free to glean away.

I swim three days a week and run one. I used to run two but made an agreement with myself to give up one day so I could use the gained day to work on this book. These days I work out with injury prevention in mind more than pace and style improvement. In comparison to my vision of a rock-star athlete, I fall significantly below that bar although I swear, I'm way faster than anyone who is not out there at all. On occasion, I have all six lanes in the pool to myself and the imagined gold medal is mine. Good for me because every swim and every run come with its challenges. So, my chosen perspective says, *I'm an athlete in process (even when I don't feel like one); to embark on a workout is not up for debate, it's just something that is a given; I can make workout swaps and cash in on earned rewards;* and, *it's the least I can do [take care of myself] in return for being given the gift of life.* My choice of commitment and dedication is based on belief, checks, balances and gratitude.

94

Meanwhile, back at the home front, all this crazy life is going on. Can be so very crazy, like when the heavy-metal, head-banging band Anthrax performs *Caught in a Mosh*. That crazy. We are constantly catching up and/or figuring out what we must do next. Resting our mind in current time becomes difficult and often unreachable. Workouts offer an ironic rest, one that gives clarity, manageability and control. When we are at mile one, three, eight or more or we are at lap one, five, thirty or more, we are present by necessity. We must be, or we run the high risk of not seeing the finish line and being off kilter while trying to head there. Being present opens a world of potential. When present, we can have much going on and be clear to move and track everything in our heads. Here's an analogous visual.

Picture this. Take Jamaica Train Station located in Queens, New York or Grand Central Terminal, New York City. I refer to these stations since I know them well. Jamaica Train Station is the largest train hub on Long Island with weekly ridership exceeding 200,000 passengers with over 1,000 trains passing through it every day. It ranks behind Pennsylvania Station, Grand Central Terminal and Secaucus Junction. Grand Central Terminal (GCT) is the largest station by number of platforms (44) that are situated on two underground levels with 41 tracks on the upper level and 26 on the lower. Side note - of the 19,000 items that are collected in the Lost and Found at GCT each year, the most unusual items include a basset hound, a pair of prosthetic earlobes, and a dead man's ashes (left there on purpose by his widow as he had used the excuse of falling asleep on the train to cover his extramarital affairs). This Lost and Found digression has nothing to do with the analogy of train hubs in relation to the mind-benefits of exercise, but it called to be included . . . smiley-face. The flippin widow left her husband's ashes riding around on the train. The visual just cracks me up. Back to the other mind visual where platforms,

95

levels, and activity exist in abundance. Enter – the state of being present in this kind of environment. Here is when a world of potential can be unleashed.

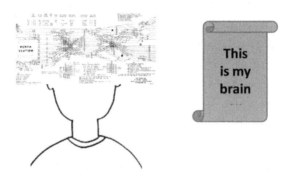

Intentionally, I've not read up on what specifically happens with the brain when it is in a present state. That is best left to the behavioral psychologists. I can only suggest that for me, being present offers expansion in my ability to stay foundational while managing and growing the many tracks that have brought and are bringing me places. Like Jamaica Train Station and GCT. Running, swimming, or whatever is our consistent, physical outlet allows us to rely on our home-base (hub) where we can see more clearly and take and manage more steps deliberately and confidently. In movement, I write mental memos, plan and determine action, dream, prioritize, make peace with conflict, create and imagine, and convinced myself to write a book.

Considering that minds have many platforms and tracks running trains in and out of our stations, it is the workout that can help to manage this mass transit situation because it forces us to be present. In a workout we can't be any further along than where we are, and we can't be behind either. When there [present], we can open head space through this state of focus. If we sit in a dark, quiet room and only stare at the flame of a candle, this openness can occur, although it is absent of needed physical movement. Being present expands the ability to become more highly functional with greater sense, order, and direction.

Many times, I hear people say that they are too busy and therefore can't find the time to exercise. I once said that (and meant it) only to be met with, "There are people out there busier than you that are getting in their work-outs". Well that certainly stopped me in my tracks! There are far too many exercise options for us to ever use *busy* as an excuse. BTW, never underestimate the benefits of even a simple walking regime.

Other reliefs about workouts. They are rarely as bad as we anticipate them to be. In fact, they are not bad at all and they charge us up. It's quite ridiculous how we can make a workout to be monumental yet when complete the deal was not so big and, what are we left with? We are left standing there with blood flowing and we are holding a sack full of benefits. Like any habit, this addiction will grab us but this one will catapult us out to a life we want and choose to live because simply put, we feel better. We become open and then realize that the new level of operating becomes the starting point for something even better. There's nothing like being on a run and mid-way it starts to rain. Just beautiful. To start a run in the rain? Well . . . that's just bad-a**.

Maybe this expanded use of the mind can be achieved without a work-out regime. Perhaps. I for one can't function toward my potential effectiveness and state of personal fulfillment without it. Workouts can give the mind a rest.

Speaking of rest, the pièce de résistance one is . . . sleep. With this, the nervous system is relatively inactive, postural muscles relax and consciousness is practically suspended. Clearly, the right amount of sleep for each of us is needed – not too much – not too little. Amounts of this necessary part of life can close on our deals or break them. Sleep is a horribly worrisome and real issue for many. Consider this. The right amount and quality of sleep will more easily follow an all-inclusive, healthy life situation. We can sleep when we are calm. The reverse is true. We can be content [in our lives] when we get enough sleep. I venture to say that our nutritional choice plan works both ways as well. We feel good when we eat right, and we eat right when we feel good. Whether it be nutrition or sleep, the focus belongs on our optimal health condition and not on one meal or one good night's sleep. We can be chefs and not short-order cooks when making self-care choices. We can operate deliberately and thoughtfully while listening inwardly and free of any self-judgement. We can hear, liberate, and step forward.

The Heart

So, what about the heart? This muscular organ pumps blood through the blood vessels of our circulatory systems. The blood provides our bodies with oxygen and nutrients and assists in the removal of metabolic wastes. It is easy to see why this headquarters of the body has also come to mean the headquarters of our feeling selves. That's the heart where we can let ourselves care. Caring is a delicate matter, opening us up to both love and pain. The heart . . . where we can receive, shield, give, deny, and grow.

The word *care* in Old English means *sorrow, anxiety, grief*. Let's use the 1580's version meaning *matter of concern, take in hand*. We are at work. We can think we care about some things and not care about other things. In pressure situations we experience others and ourselves exclaiming we don't care about this or that. Of the few basic and pure truths in life, care must be one of them. We load it up with rights we think we have on it. Meanwhile care is just care like love is just love. We don't have ownership of it although we can think we do.

"From caring comes courage."
–Lao Tzu

Take this book. I do care about what people will think of it. I do care about what people think in general. Just because I care does not mean that I'll necessarily concern myself with other's reactions. Depends – correct? Although feedback can be intellectual nourishment it does not need to, nor should, ever serve to diminish our foundational selves.

And Who Am I? Wrap-Up

Mind. Drive. Body. Heart. Visualize osmosis. Osmosis is a process by which molecules of a solvent tend to pass through a semipermeable membrane from a less concentrated solution into a more concentrated one, thus equalizing the concentrations on each side of the membrane. It's also the process of gradual or unconscious assimilation of ideas and knowledge.

Balance in motion. When mind, drive, body, and heart are in an osmotic state we've got it going on . . . big time.

Let the Sunshine in . . .
the Su –u –n – Shine in!

This balanced state can make room for us to perform well and grow. This *space* is valuable, prime real estate. What can we do with this added capacity? Well, Assistants have the advantage of an organizational-wide view. Additionally, we can see from the top down so basically that includes everything. We continuously build two-way bridges for bosses and people, people and other people and outsiders and insiders. This can be enough to manage in our workdays but for some of us it might not fully quench our thirst. We are in a great position to be visionary and with some added *space*, we can create and develop. We have ideas and we see opportunities. For me, I've taken on the overhaul and maintenance of an internal communication directory (approximately 30 departments), participated in cancer care 35 mile walks, updated the communications/switchboard office (as you can imagine no small task), was part of a conference room scheduling initiative, coordinated an annual ice-cream social, streamlined the mail room office, volunteered where I could, organized a support group directory, am writing a book, and every window sill in the administration office and conference room holds orchid plants (aka the ICU for orchids) where people can bring their waning orchids for a chance at new life. These extras help to fulfill my sense of community and personal input within the work environment.

I know a musician who developed a food collection service for the hungry; I know an Assistant who helps both teens and adults with writing their first resumes; I know a physician who started a 5K Run to benefit women and men serving our country; I know a vice president who organizes an annual Independence Day float; I know a mother who began a local non-profit mental health network organization that focuses on education, outreach and support for local families; I know an editor who dog walks with the physically challenged; I know four Assistants who, without hesitation, dipped into their own pockets to tip a truck driver who arrived on the wrong day; I know a clerk who tutors kids in math; I know a healer who donates her time to those in need who have no money to spend on their well-being; I know an exercise physiologist who holds a volunteer trustee spot in local government; I know a medical sales technologist who took the plunge and opened a music school for kids while he maintains his full time job and raises two young children; I know a teacher who created an after-school yoga class for kids in warm months and a cross-county skiing class in cold months and another teacher who takes the time to work on the accounting and preservation of cemetery tombstones for people who date back to the mid-18th century; I know a facilities manager who is on call to rescue wildlife; I know of a software engineer who has figured out how to have a sixteen year-old paraplegic girl open and close her bedroom door by only using her sight and a computer; and, I know a man who runs a conflict resolution camp in Maine for kids from varied Middle East countries and is in his 25th year of doing so.

"Inspiration, move me brightly. Light the song with sense and color. Hold away despair."
- Grateful Dead

We can indeed be incredibly amazing.

Throughout my growing years, I remember my mother consistently expressing four major convictions: the sacredness of and the unwavering rights to our personal and physical bodies, the importance of being our own best friend, especially when we need it the most, the knowing that our reserves are deeper than we may think, and the ultimate power of faith. This self-care advice is mint. We are all worthy of a commitment to looking after ourselves.

What we want to do and who we want to be can be who we are.

Mind . . . Drive . . . Body . . . Heart.

"The cave you fear to enter holds the treasure you seek. Own the fear, find the cave, and write a new ending for yourself, for the people you are meant to serve and support. Choose courage over comfort and choose the great adventure of being brave, and afraid, at the exact same time."
-Joseph Campbell

101

CHAPTER 9

Proactive Anticipation during Changing Tides

While hindsight can teach us much, the ability to predict and the action of forecasting will keep us on the front line. We are then able to both stand and turn curves with leadership on missions. We are part of the team that can realize what was once but a vision. Most of us in our jobs help to improve lives whether it is through education, entertainment, health, rights, building and maintenance, transportation, security, and any type of work where progress for improvement is involved. We are also part of the team that at times can find ourselves *in irons*. This state describes a trapped condition that a sailing ship finds itself in when the bow of the ship is heading into the wind and the ship has stalled and is unable to come about or tack either way. Leadership and others figure it out and tides change. Optimized Assistants are adept at thinking out-of-the-box and can and hopefully do offer solution-based ideas that stem from our insights. We are pillars, propping and supporting institutions.

"Oh the places you'll go! There is fun to be done! There are
points to be scored. There are games to be won.
And the magical things you can do with that ball will make you
the winning-est winner of all."
-Dr. Seuss, Oh, The Places You'll Go!

Assistants equip because essentially that is our job, but proactive readiness does more than one might think. Our boss asks us to print out an updated committee list in preparation for a meeting that will be taking place in an hour with both the board and governance/nominating chairs. We don't need to be told why the committee list is requested. We also do not have to ask because we are in tune and can figure this out because the annual meeting is days away. We print out three copies for all meeting participants instead of the requested one and avoid the inevitable request for more. As minor as this may seem, if this take-charge method is our general operating mode, we then gain and maintain an advantage in situations. We also affect perceptions. We help others to have confidence in leadership because their experience is that of our consistent preparedness and reliability.

Here's another example of proactive readiness. We are at the onset of a board meeting and the report of the medical staff follows the approval of the minutes from the prior meeting. Although the attendance of the chair of the medical staff is expected, we take note that she is not present, likely due to her primary role as physician in the emergency department. The scenario will play out and a back-up reporting plan will occur. Fine. No big deal. Perhaps slight, it is nevertheless an interruption. Here is what works better. While the minute's motion is being made, seconded and approved, we equip our boss with medical staff report in hand and a whisper of the absence. No beat missed. Movement. Movement. Movement. Board members have confidence in leadership when stops, starts, and delays are avoided. Assistants who anticipate and respond keep motion fluid so that all can maintain focus and carry on with the business at hand.

I won't bore us with anticipation stories since that is our basic operating system of awake life.

Let's talk about what happens between anticipation and proactivity for the Assistant. Anticipate then act. It can sound so simple and at times, it is. But my, oh my, oh my - many times the action part can be quite the hard-read. Sometimes we end up in a roll-the-dice decision. Should I? Shouldn't I? Is the time now, maybe not? Is it ever? Is it my role? Am I over-stepping? Is my perspective on point? Is this a real priority or a poser priority? If it's a priority to me, but not to my boss, how do I handle that? Do I have an obligation? These are just some of the questions we have throughout our days as Assistant. It is not all defined for us . . . is it. (This is meant as a statement and not a question.) There are too many scenarios and too many temperaments involved. How we choose to take action becomes rather intricate and certainly personal. If you are new to the role, make like a sponge and absorb until you are saturated. That is a good point to begin to exercise the *When/How/If* factor. We can then better determine our moves. No point in jumping the gun. If proactive decisions are made before we are really ready to make them, it will become a restart or a disqualification for us. *When/How/If* to take initiative . . . there lies the question. It takes necessary time and experience for us to get a good measure on our *taking action* decisions. There is a rigid dichotomy between driven energy and patience, yet coupled together, they become a winning ticket. As time does its thing . . . (you know, the thing that only time can do), we become more comfortable. Our confidence levels boldly lead us directly to anticipating and then acting in appropriate and proactive ways. My decisions regarding proactivity twenty-seven years in are quite different from when I was a newcomer. There have been 9,855 days of experience and growth, both difficult and incredible. If we honor where we are in our process, then we can trust both our abilities to anticipate and our decisions to take action. We will not get too far ahead of ourselves, nor will we lag. If we want to streamline our own growth, we need to surf our own wave.

"Well," said Pooh, "what I like best," and then he had to stop and think. Because although Eating Honey was a very good thing to do, there was a moment just before you begin to eat it which was better than when you were, but he didn't know what it was called.

-A.A. Milne, Winnie-the-Pooh

Optimized Assistants anticipate and act. It takes much synchronization and patience to have these critical-to-success traits under our belts. I wonder if we forget at times to feel good about the moment just before we eat the honey.

CHAPTER 10

The Assistant/Boss Relationship

Well . . . they certainly do come in all shapes and leadership styles – don't they! Furthermore, management approach is unique to each one of them.

"Let's start at the very beginning. A very good place to start."
-Do-Re-Mi, The Sound of Music

Approaching our Assistant/Boss relationships from the vantage points of gaining education, providing service, maintaining shelter, obtaining health care and other benefits, and acquiring food for nourishment, can set a solid foundation for how we perceive and cope with the Assistant/Boss relationship. The approach of gratitude keeps us focused on progress and minimizes the risks of getting caught up in psychological frustrations. When frustrations are replaced with gratefulness, we work with clarity, peace of mind, and happiness.

First, to work with purpose is a beautiful thing. That being said and absorbed, through work Assistants are gifted with an incredible education, and we are paid for it. According to the *U.S. News and World Report*, in the United States the average cost of tuition and fees for the 2018-2019 school year was $9,716 for state residents at public colleges, $21,629 for out-of-state residents attending public universities, and $35,676 for those attending private colleges. This is per year. It is fair to say that my 27 years of work equals either $262,332, $583,983, or $963,252 worth of schooling that I have been paid for in both money and health benefits. How's that for investment and accomplishment? Congratulations to all of you who have been paid for your good work, your education, and your health and other benefits.

Secondly, to be able to work is good fortune. According to the *Bureau of Labor Statistics*, in the United States, there is currently a 3.7% (12,175,401.9 individuals) unemployment rate as of August 2019. Syria has the highest unemployment rate at 50%. It is daunting to peruse unemployment rates of some of the 195 countries in today's world. For the employed, both inward and outward expressions of dissatisfaction or annoyance about work can seep in. Walk in the shoes of someone out of work. Well, let's think twice before we complain about our jobs.

The basic point here is this: Entering our workday with gratitude sets a stage for rightmindedness.

Despite this foundational approach, relationships can become complicated, including those with our bosses. We have already covered difficult relationship tactics (see Chapter 3, *Assistant to Assistant Relationships*). These approaches work with all individuals and in varied situations. Two things to add here regarding the Assistant/Boss relationship. First, there is a heightened level that can be challenging to this relationship simply because we work so closely together and our boss relies on us directly, often the posthaste type of reliance. Since our boss is our immediate report, there are little or no varying levels of authority to dialogue with or represent ourselves on our behalf, if we think we need that. Therefore, mutual respect and cooperative interactions are of paramount importance. Secondly, we know better than just about anyone that our boss's time is restricted, and that often her/his focus is that of an airplane's view at thirty thousand feet. Contrary to what may seem a logical given to many, we know that bosses are not always available to us. When everyone and everything is a priority to them, we must figure out our standing in that sea of needs. Although we serve as gatekeeper, we line ourselves up accordingly, and frequently defer to others first. Often, it is we who must wait, and we must manage this time with toleration and understanding. The position requires us to create and form our own identity while identifying with all. We are part of no one, yet one of everyone.

As I reflect on past bosses I've had in all jobs since I was sixteen years old, I realize that the education never stopped, regardless of any struggles I had or struggles an organization had with the boss or leadership, or with me. It is often by way of those trying times that we can experience the rising of the phoenix, the reinvention of the heart of an organization, and of ourselves. Although by no means easy, these valuable lessons should not be underestimated or underappreciated. Ideally, they should be honored.

Yes, we can make generalizations, be affected by perceptions of others, and draw conclusions prematurely, but we can also choose to step back and absorb the situations we have when working so closely with our boss. And there it is. Time and consideration. Observation so that we can mentally withdraw from personal or organizational conflict in order to consider matters objectively. This is not always easy when we are managing our own selves while being our Assistant selves. Nevertheless, it sure beats holding court in a tangled web.

Although navigating through challenging boss relationships can affect our quality of life, take the time to stop, drop, and roll.

We don't need to fuel the fire. Use objectivity to our favor. Let's take a moment to realize that persevering through difficult phases teaches us much, as long as we keep the health of ourselves and of our organizations in focus. Let's be good students and not deny ourselves an education. Instead, let's choose (yes there is that word choose again) to only be part of solutions.

So easy for me at this particular point in my career to write about the benefits of appreciating a boss.

Number Seven. My current boss. I've come to find out that the number seven both in Mandarin and Cantonese symbolizes *togetherness* and is a lucky number for relationships. It is also recognized as the luckiest number in the West. People have named taverns, movies, casinos, laundromats, breweries, trucking companies, hotels, mini-marts, and television shows "Lucky Seven".

I clearly recall the point in time when I was ready to leave the years of laboring through administration transitions and work with and for someone that I could help plant flags. I got extremely lucky, maybe a bit by chance, but more so by how a Roman philosopher, statesman, dramatist and satirist of the Silver Age of Latin literature viewed luck:

"Luck is what happens when preparation meets opportunity."
-Lucius Annaeus Seneca

So yes, I got lucky and my adventures to work with a phenomenal boss took hold.

Great bosses, like Number Seven, are also great people. They are honest, good listeners, inspirational, insightful, forward thinking, fair, and considerate. They foster work, people, and life balance. Hopefully they are funny. And yes, they are human and are subject to all that comes with that. The simple beautiful result of working with and for a great boss is that work life, which can affect non-work life, is far more enjoyable. Although education transpires regardless of the Assistant/Boss relationship, the great boss one generally moves in the direction of feel-good betterment. Even our great boss relationships have times of frustration and this can basically be due to opposing emotional mindsets at any given time. Boss takes a moment to share something funny or interesting and although that is so very great, go figure, it comes at a time where we are working in a pressure cooker. And the reverse occurs. We are really excited and begin to share our new granola recipe success story and suddenly we realize boss is in data analyzing mode. And what about when our boss is having a hectic day and we are managing a rough one ourselves? These dynamics are all part of human interaction and as the international bestselling author, activist, and social entrepreneur Bryant McGill states, *"There is a simple path to follow that appears only when you calm your mind"*. Thank you, Bryant, – that is great advice.

Employment, service, and education aside, consider the following three necessary anchors for the *"start at the beginning"* mind-set regarding Assistant/Boss relationships.

Loyalty – Old French *loial* meaning *of good quality, faithful, honorable.*

Allegiance – from Anglo-French *legaunce* meaning *ties or obligation of a citizen or subject to a government or sovereign.*

Devotion – Ancient Latin *devotionem*, meaning *act of consecrating by a vow.*

Having these attributes as footings for our growing relationships with our bosses not only keeps us thinking in similar ways but also continuously re-establishes respect and reason for effort. It allows two people, Leader and Assistant, to act in concert toward progress, sustainability, and attainment, each exercising their dissimilar areas of expertise for the same goal. It's the crunchy peanut butter with the jelly, the popcorn with the movie, the fish with the chips, it's the Lone Ranger and Tonto.

"Hi-Yo, Silver! Away!"

Assistants on occasion can be in a position where we need to ask our boss a timely question while they are in, let's say . . . an off-site lunch meeting. Ugh. Ok. Hmmmm. Decision made. We know it is important. Thank you Finnish engineer Matti Makkonen for conceiving of the text message idea (that was eight years prior to the actual first text message sent on December 3, 1992). The texting option is an Assistant's superhero when working with bosses. It's 12:17pm. We text, *"important-will you be able to call back Lily Squoxy before 12:45?"* Return response. *"yes. don't I have a 12:30?"* Our response back. *"ooops, yes. u might be able to get her at the end of the day-stay tuned. It's the east satellite case."* This quick text dialogue establishes: 1, something needs to happen that won't happen until later in the day. 2, what the subject is. 3, we missed something but are already in recovery mode. Movement. Preparation. Provision. *Provision* – Latin meaning *foresee* and Old French to English, meaning *foresight*. These nouns keep our game on offense. We are driving and not in park nor in neutral. Sorry for the interruption boss and thanks for understanding. We've gained more than lost, plus your lunch can carry on, and now so can we.

Ahhhhhhhh yes . . . the need to interrupt our boss. I imagine we have consensus on how we feel about this unfortunate bear-of-a-job responsibility. We have got to do it so let's try to make the best of it. Here are a few options I have pulled from my inventory. I must add, these interrupt choices are not random. They are chosen carefully depending on the specific situation.

When boss is in a meeting and texting is not an option:

- There is the enter room . . . head down . . . no eye-contact . . . drop a post it note direct to boss . . . and back out in reverse option. (When I do this, I imagine the beep-beep sound that vehicles make when backing-up);
- There is the enter the room . . . head up . . . make eye-contact . . . drop a post-it note direct to boss . . . wait a couple of seconds to determine if the FYI is enough or if boss opts to give direction . . . then about-face . . . walk out assuredly . . . and stay on our mission option;
- There is the enter the room . . . with the *oh-so-sorry-but-I-have-to-interrupt* face option;
- There is the above option but then add a tiny sense of annoyance if you are looking for a quicker response;
- There is the enter the room . . . head up . . . with facial expression that says *this is the last thing I want to be doing at this point so please figure I'm here because it is the right thing not the desired thing* option;
- There is the open the door. . . don't enter the room . . . spot out boss and do the index-finger, *come-out-here* motion option (adding a half-smile makes this not rude);
- There is the open the door . . . make eye-contact with boss . . . and stand there completely motionless because boss already knows why we are there option;
- There is the open the door . . . don't enter the room . . . spot out and give boss the inquisitive face while our palms of hands are face up and add the quick point to an invisible watch on our wrist option.

113

I imagine it's important to cater our interrupt option choices to what works with our specific situations. That being said, Assistants, don't be afraid. We interrupt because we must. It is a very positive sign if our bosses trust that when we appear at non-invited meetings, functions, events, etc., they know we are doing our jobs and doing them well. Like Shakespeare's most frequently quoted passage, *"All the world's a stage..."*, we are well cast and qualified to play our part emphatically.

Assistants operate from many angles when dealing with bosses, one of which is the caboose of a train. A caboose is a railroad car, coupled at the end of a North American freight train. It provides shelter for crew who are required for switching and shunting, damage to equipment and cargo, and overheating axles. In other words, it is where conflict is avoided. Yes . . . Assistants own the caboose.

Being a caboose is a great way to serve our boss well. We are in a high-level meeting. A new piece of equipment is mentioned and after its description and purpose are stated, our boss says that we will coordinate a day and time for meeting attendees to tour the department. This offer can easily be overlooked in the enormous amount of follow through items that occur each day. Assistant, jot it down and remind later. Conflict avoided. At a department head meeting, our boss refers to an article and notes we will distribute it. Assistant, jot it down and remind (or distribute) later. Conflict avoided. This follow-through helps to foster faith and reliability as action items are stated and promises are made.

Here's another example, via email from an Assistant in caboose-mode. *"Boss, just to confirm, as you mentioned in Strategic Planning on Friday, should I be sending the attached to Board members? If so, they should be warned that it is 198 pages. Also, aside from saying what it is and that it's for their information, is there anything else you want added in the note?"* So, Assistants, bring up the rear. Close the loop. Fly like the crow. Encompass. *Encompass* - Middle English meaning, *surround and have or hold within.*

Having organizational awareness is a jewel in our crown and complements the Assistant/Boss relationship. Moreover, it will make our job more interesting and we become more helpful because we have increased our knowledge base and hence, we now have a public relations skill. Just the other day, I was at the post office and had an eight-minute wait for it to open. Within that time, I educated three also-waiting people on the status of the cancer center project and the new hospital facility building project. They left in good thoughts and I left as a fulfilled walking advertisement. We can speak to our business's mission, vision, values, and progress. This is important because Assistants represent both the individual and the entity. Operating from a broad picture view while drilling down to many specifics will keep us well rounded and challenged. The word *know* is Germanic in origin and in Old English is defined as *recognize, identify.* So, *knowing* requires action. Go for it.

Active knowing calls for alert senses. Alert senses help us to optimize ourselves. Recently moths have been named as having the best hearing in the world. This may be due to having to evade threat of their major predator, the bat. The eyesight of birds (eagles, hawks, buzzards) is 3-4 times sharper than ours. Insects have the best motion detectors; they have compound eyes that can have hundreds of lenses that each sees a little bit of the overall picture. An amalgamation of the moth/bird/insect would make a phenomenal Assistant. Keeping our senses alert will increase our rate of knowledge absorption and our potential for decisive action.

Meet MIB . . . Assistant Extraordinaire

Assistant/Boss Relationship Wrap-Up

OK. There are lengthy guidebooks written on Assistant/Boss relationships that some of us may find useful. In my opinion, what has changed from the 1960s is the Assistant role, not the Assistant/ Boss relationship. Certainly, there are, in present times, different sets of circumstances that affect the relationship. The intricacies of relationships exist regardless of specific circumstances. We get along well with others or we don't. Since I like to keep things basic, the health of an Assistant/Boss relationship is rooted in mutual respect. Absent of this shared sentiment, we have a choice. Figure it out or find something that we think is more suited for us. Mutual respect occurs when both individuals work with purpose and gratitude, and the Assistant honors the three sacred anchors of loyalty, allegiance, and devotion. Maybe it can be called professional maturity or maybe it's optimization at work. As for we Assistants, our job, at minimum, is to clear obstacles so that our bosses can take care of their responsibilities. Organizational awareness elevates our abilities to clear the obstacles. Let's honor where we are in our own growth so that we can continue to add to our self and organizational value. We need to own a high level of tact and independence. It is an interesting place to be and one where we need to hold profound confidences on each end of a burning candle. We anticipate. We envision. We respond. We shake. We pour. So, antennas up Assistants. A really awesome person/ professional I know recently said about us, "You do play in the big leagues. Your collective poise, leadership, and trust is required."

CHAPTER 11
Whose Crisis is it Anyway?

Not ours.

At times, Assistants are confronted by people in heavy-duty crisis mode. Chapter 6, *Communication in Difficult Situations,* suggests some response strategies.

Crisis in late Middle English denotes the *turning point of a disease.* Not good. Let's not go there.

Chapter over.

CHAPTER 12

Flippin' Funny

What is this word funny? In the 1680s it meant *to cheat*. In 1806 it meant *strange* and in 1833 meant *to make fun, jest, joke*. Funny can also mean underhanded, as in, *something funny about those extra charges*, which is not really funny at all. Funny in the best sense of the word means laugh and the sudden and uncontrollable type of laugh can rank supreme. This good type of funny boldly stands up to pressure and wins every single time. This chapter relates to the happy funny.

Humor plays on human reactions in all sorts of ways. What is very funny to some is not that funny to others. Even when something is funny to a group of people, there are varying degrees of response. Comic expression comes in many forms: anecdotal, off-color, dark, farcical, satirical, dry, and situational, just to name a few. Regardless, humor is a lifeline when we need to balance out difficult circumstances and it's an enhancer, even when we are riding high.

I remember a game my four siblings and I would play as kids. Someone would start by slowly saying, "ah ha ha ha ha", and then repeating it. Others would chime in on the monotonous and boring-sounding mantra. In a matter of seconds, our facial expressions would become skewed and distorted and we would soon all be uncontrollably and hysterically laughing. Yes, laughter is exceptionally good medicine.

Words themselves can be funny. Funny how we can dust strawberries and also dust tables. We can execute both a document and a person. We can safely buckle up and we can also buckle under pressure and collapse. We can assemble papers with a clip, and we can disassemble shrubs with a clip. We can be happily outstanding and then have something regretfully outstanding. We can be finished and completed or finished and destroyed. A pig can be in a pen and we can also write with a pen. A dog can bark at a tree that has bark. We can tire while pushing a tire. We can drive on a parkway and we can park on a driveway. These contronyms, aka auto-antonyms, and homonyms, I find f-u-n-n-y. Funny sparks all kinds of faces and affects everyone differently. It can be shared and also intimately personal. Funny is a relief.

An Assistant is trying to get to the gym after work and while multi-tasking, she inadvertently leaves her hair straightener in her boss's office. Funny when he found it. Co-worker walks into a wall. Funny. A woman's heel lodges in a crack as she exits an elevator and walks out of her stiletto. Funny. It's still funny as I recall a school superintendent waiting to meet with the boss and she helps herself to snacks that were in a bowl, but what she ate was potpourri. Kid you not, these are all true incidences. Humor humanizes.

Some things are not funny at the time but very funny later . . . like when the parade committee was painstakingly looking to locate the big cooler that holds water bottles for the marchers and come to find out, it had promptly been used to transport a body part in ice to an emergency room (successful outcome by the way). Or what about when an Assistant looked in on a meeting being held between her boss and the board chair and they had helped themselves to water. Thing is, they had taken two tumbler-type glasses that were in fact, flower vases. Or take the teacher who kept clarifying to a third grader that he could not go to the beach because it was school-time and not beach-time, and the kid was simply letting him know that he needed to go to speech, not beach. What about the Assistant who threads through the days mail in a *when-in-doubt-throw-it-out* mode. The value of the $30K check ripped in half soon equaled zero. Funny now. An Assistant mistakenly gives the same meeting dial-in information to both the marketing/advertising and finance/budget committees. Same day, same time, both committees dialed in simultaneously. Let's just say the marketing and advertising members were opportunistic and the finance and budget members not so much. Not at all funny at the time yet very funny now.

There is an Assistant who cracks a joke to her under-pressure boss. He laughs. Success. "Take 2" and he can begin again, minus angst. Re-starts and do-overs are necessary when trying to balance progression with agitated types of emotions. To clarify this point, consider projects as enterprises. Take films. They often require multiple takes. Director Stanley Kubrick had Shelley Duvall repeat a scene 127 times for *The Shining*. Charlie Chaplin, both director and star of *The Gold Rush*, did 63 separate takes of a scene where his character eats a boot. Side note: the boot prop was made of licorice and Chaplin ended up in the hospital for insulin shock due to high sugar intake. One fight scene in Jackie Chan's *The Young Master* was so intricate that it required 329 takes to complete. Our workdays can require multiple takes and humor can be just the switch we need.

To re-start we have options to consider. We can walk it off, meditate it out, pray, hang tough and work through it, find the lighter side of a situation, or stay ticked and wait it out. We can also choose to laugh. Find the funny. Researchers have studied and philosophers have theorized much about laughter. There's a whole world of explanations, benefits, causes, types, and research that dissects all aspects of laughing. Bottom line, there is something about laughter that remarkably resets perspective. Laughter is ours for the giving and for the taking.

There is a boss who when pressures became intense, would break out his harmonica and play a few tunes. There is a father who bakes and creates while whistling to counteract downward child-rearing spirals. When confusion sets in, there is an engineer who tends to her vegetable garden while listening to comic podcasts and then enjoys her crops from ground to table. There is a student who in the midst of exam study, sings and dances in her living room as if it's the performance of her life. In 1991, there was a couple who during their wedding ceremony stated their marriage vows and when it came time to light the unity candle, no flame . . . broken. Fortunately, I found this very funny as opposed to telling, and with a big smile, asked the congregation, *does anyone have a light?* Thirty years later, marriage intact - whew. Yes, laughter cuts through tense situations. It's 8:00am. A director walks out of the rest room and realizes the copy machine is finally available and exclaims, "You go to the bathroom for sixty seconds and the world can change!" Cracked me up. And good morning!

An Assistant walks into her office and her boss of over twelve years walks out of his and asks, "Where's the paper?" Only Assistants will really get the humor in that.

If we find ourselves on the drive home from work, unwinding as we must, and suddenly feel the smile on our face and hear the laugh from our mouth as we recall an incident or situation from

124

our day, then let's just say that in the divine order of things, all is very good.

So, what does this word funny do? Funny is a nice surprise we unexpectedly get or deliberately give that cuts through all that is stressful. We can create the laugh and we can receive the laugh. We can find the laugh. What we don't want to do, though, is miss the laugh.

CHAPTER 13

Ultimate Job Satisfaction and the Importance of Validation

While the importance of satisfaction in job success is obvious, validation solidifies our efforts and accomplishments by shutting ready-to-close doors and unlocking ready-to-open doors. Let's look at both satisfaction and validation separately and then see how they work in close association.

Satisfaction - Latin *satisfacere* meaning *content*. The earliest recorded use of this word satisfy referred to the last part of religious penance after confession, and it involved fulfillment of the observance required by the confessor. In some contrast to the current meaning, today we see satisfaction as *fulfillment of one's own expectations*.

We cannot fake fulfillment. Just not possible. Taking the time to privately and broadly think about our self-expectations can help us to gauge, monitor, and do something about our levels of satisfaction. We can be quick to say we are not satisfied, almost as if the feeling of discontent was bestowed upon us by something other than ourselves.

A daughter told her mother that she hung up from an infuriating phone call with her manager. Apparently, she found out that every member of her team, except for her, was involved in the development of a big idea deck for a client. The reasons stated were higher-level budget restrictions of some sort. She texts her mother, *"I'm better than this . . . why does everyone keep trying to kill my creative flame?"* Mother texts back, *"Don't know, but consensus can move mountains - even our own. Your answer can begin there."* (The power of consensus is detailed in Chapter 5.) Taking accountability for the pickles we find ourselves in is an important first step to conflict resolution and eventual satisfaction. Next, establishing mutual understanding through sound communication opens options for inclusion or for new opportunities. Satisfaction is in reach when we break out of our disappointment shell and view what is actually out there.

In our jobs (and in our lives), we can become our own obstacles and then wonder why things don't work out for us. Tying self-belief to our sense of self-expectation can make headway toward fulfillment. None of this is new. I just wonder how we weigh out the time we take with ourselves before we arrive at the self-related conclusions that we draw, and thereby, we miss the step of honest and personal fulfillment discovery. We can forget to add the <u>not</u> after the <u>why</u>.

Validation - In the 1570's the word valid meant *having force in law, legally binding,* and from Middle French *valide* (16c.) and Latin *validus*, it meant *strong, effective, powerful, active.* The word was first recorded in 1640 as *sufficiently supported by facts or authority, well grounded.* The *–tion* suffix forms it as a noun of action, condition, etc. There are multitudes of synonyms for the word validation and the common ones include *authenticate, approve, endorse, acceptance, testament,* and *affirmation.*

Logic dictates that validation happens after satisfaction is realized by our own selves and/or others. Example: A leader of an organization envisions and effectuates a sustainable new program. Self-fulfillment for the leader. Responses and reactions follow, and validation shows a signed, sealed, and delivered reward. Some form of respect and acknowledgement is given to the leader from those whose work lives have been improved or whose lives have been improved, and it all began with the leader's vision, implementation, and self-belief. Satisfaction and validation marry nicely here.

Although it is really nice to receive acknowledgement from others, validation can also exist absent of feedback. Yes, there is the ever-important self-validation, but there is also the unspoken knowing that some act we completed was validated. Consider the following anecdotes as they clearly show satisfaction, yet they also come full circle and attest to and authenticate the act itself. Validation.

Earlier in this book, (Chapter 6, *Communication*), there is a reference to a barge that was sinking in the Atlantic Ocean and medical supplies were needed. The point related to handling rapid thought and decisive action. This very real story importantly belongs in this chapter as well. On April 24, 2017, the Coast Guard stated the need for Lactated Ringers IV Solution for an emergency and in a matter of minutes, 60 (1,000cc) and 72 (500cc) bags were on their way to those in need. Perhaps the difference between the *earned income/sense of purpose* benefits of job satisfaction, and the experience of ultimate job-satisfaction, is that moment where we become selfless. That moment where we experience the rightness of life and our motive is self-effacing and our demeanor and heart are gracious. Validation.

In a 12-story office building people waited for the elevator in the main lobby. Bing . . . it arrived, doors opened and there stood a little boy alone in the elevator. He must have been around six years old and was frightened and cried. He must have entered on whatever floor and hit a button. To the concierge, keeping this kid safe was the job at hand while convincing him he was amongst friends made the difference to the boy. It's the human connections we pay attention to that can often lead us to the encounter with ultimate job satisfaction. Validation.

In a gym locker room, there was an adorable little girl who was clearly hesitant to exit the locker room and enter the pool area. She was shy, scared, and intimidated. By chance, the coach entered the locker room and after short dialogue realized the little girl's self-consciousness and fear. Yes, the coach's job was to teach swimming but the job that made the difference was to put her at ease and share the reassuring and confident high-five. That moment was that coach's ultimate job satisfaction. Validation.

I was in the hustle and bustle of the city just the other day. I watched a sewage treatment worker hoist himself out of a manhole to help a blind person cross the street. Perhaps this was the worker's ultimate job satisfaction that day. Validation.

There are many opportunities we can take that can cross the line from job satisfaction to utmost rightness. Whether we are at work or not, tending to those in need or crisis elevates our response factor and sense of fulfillment. We can be doing something important and suddenly we find ourselves involved with something even more important like getting meds to a barge, instilling belief and confidence in a child, and offering a hand and eyes for someone without.

There are other ways to realize ultimate job satisfaction aside from those times born from need or crisis. What about the time an Assistant transferred an offshore satellite call from a husband to a wife post-surgery? Phone receiver was back in place and a silent moment of pure goodness occurred. Or the time an Assistant was sitting in a board retreat during immense change, already privy to the topics and statuses, and self-noted that it was quite an honor to be present. He left the retreat in awe of witnessing leaders of healthcare process change in action. Or what about the Assistant who took a moment during a tough day to acknowledge that all the work she did led to smooth operations and established the reputation and viability of an organization? What about the Assistant who unknowingly, at the time, motivated a colleague to better herself? Ultimate job satisfaction. Validation.

As Assistants, we are well positioned to have far-reaching access to all kinds of people and options. From desire, belief, and vision, we can push limits. We can also keep channels clear and help others fly by. We can also be counted as part of an initiative that only core teams can accomplish. We can be enterprising, and our role is saturated with opportunities.

Maybe ultimate job satisfaction and validation comes to us as we sit on our deck or at our kitchen table with our dog, or a child, or a sibling, or a partner, or a parent, or a friend, or we are alone, and we breathe in only appreciation.

CHAPTER 14
Closing/Opening

The optimized Assistant's desk is never clear of work and looking for something to do is never the experience. As challenging and as trying as the position can be, it offers a silver lining, which importantly references hope that difficult times always lead to better days. Our role offers us even more. It provides that blank canvas for us to create our own masterpiece. It gives us a chance to liberate and excel while on our own unique journeys. It's on these journeys where we can grow and give. We can crank it up . . . we can calm it down . . . we can share . . . we can influence. Career-based shared education. The hidden treasures will become clear. YES.

"Whether or not we can understand one another linguistically, culturally, and emotionally, if we can all have an immovable conviction in our worthiness to occupy the human heart, then naturally we will feel connected."
-Sakyong Mipham

It has been my pleasure to both think and write about us. Our shared Assistant role makes me warm because we have much in common and we make a difference toward betterment. Go us! I am honored to be one of all of us. As I close this out, I also open what is ahead. Choice. Charge. Ready to elevate. Ready to serve.

If music were playing as I wind down this writing, I'd choose this song for us . . . it's the exit from, and the entrance to . . . .

It's all so exciting!

Now, if you can imagine this, the whole world sharing one big kiss
These are thoughts all through my brain, that I daydream everyday
That I'm alive and well, and right now, I'm alive, I'm feeling...well
It's my life to live my way, so I'll keep daydreaming away
And who knows, maybe someday, it will all come true
And I will get my way, and we will live as one
And what cannot will be done, for every living thing under the sun
Forget color, forget race, and just be one big happy face
Among this sea of people, live among God's creatures, sharing love
That was sent down from above, here to share with one another
Father, brother, sister, mother, everybody sharing love, sharing love
What if...I close my eyes and everything will be alright
Here in my fantasy, living in harmony
Make my dream come alive
Now, if you can imagine this, the whole world sharing one big kiss
Take away the pain and hurt, make like heaven here on earth
Without reason to die, and given everlasting life for all

And here's the chorus . . .

I'm caught up in a dream, I'm gonna wish for it all
No one's gonna tell me how, no way, this is my dream now
I'm caught up in what seems simply impossible
I ain't gonna change a thing, no way, it's my dream, this is my dream
-Tesla

134

So . . . What do you get when you anticipate, envision, respond, shake, and pour?

You get us. You get Abby . . . You get Amylou . . . You get Andy . . . You get Ann . . . You get Caitlin . . . You get Carol . . . You get Chi . . . You get Claire . . . You get Coleen . . . You get Danielle . . . You get Devin . . . You get Diana . . . You get Diane . . . You get Dina . . . You get Doug . . . You get Francesca . . . You get Gayle . . . You get Geri . . . You get Gina . . . You get Heidi . . . You get Jackie . . . You get Janet . . . You get Jean . . . You get Jen . . . You get Jimmy . . . You get Kellie . . . You get Leslie . . . You get Leta . . . You get Lillian . . . You get Linda . . . You get Lindsay . . . You get Laurie . . . You get Lorraine . . . You get Marie . . . You get Marilyn . . . You get Marissa . . . You get Mary Beth . . . You get Nadia . . . You get Nagam . . . You get Neha . . . You get Nardy . . . You get Pam . . . You get Pat . . . You get Rachel . . . You get Ramona . . . You get Robin . . . You get Rosaria . . . You get Shaneen . . . You get Sharri . . . You get Sue . . . You get Susan . . . You get Tammy . . . You get Taylor . . . You get Vicky . . . You get Victor . . . You get Yvonne . . . You get Zanetta . . . You get . . . _____ . . .

With a double - high five, here's to our dreams!

To living and working in peace, Heidi

Made in the USA
Coppell, TX
09 April 2020